Breathe - Reviews

Breathe is a journey through the shallow waters of relationships, the crashing waves of leading a double life and the black deeps of depression, loneliness and despair. As most memoirs do, this book exposes the roller coaster ride of her life — but unlike most, Jones keeps the names of the others involved to herself; it's an expose, all right, but the skeletons in the closet belong to her alone. This is a tale of despair and redemption, but if you're expecting a fairy tale ending you'll miss the point. When you've plumbed the absolute depths of what you are, and confronted what you find, you have two choices: you can embrace the safety of the deep or climb to the surface and … breathe."
~Renee Struthers, East Oregonian

Breathe is a memoir that knocks the wind out of you. Reeling from the poetry-infused sucker punches delivered by Rae Jones, the reader of this memoir is left gasping between the chapters, sucked down the windpipe of her life as we watch the power of breath sustain…and destroy.
~Caelan Huntress, Creative Digital Messaging

Rae Jones, who is no relation to me, delivers the story of her life in a provocative, real and raw fashion. Yep, you want to read this book if you have ever identified with wearing masks to cover the wounds hidden in the depths.
~Mikaela Jones, Author of The Little Book of Light

Also by Rae Jones:

Books:
How to Create Wealth (2011)

How to Buy Insurance (2011)

How to Overcome Stress (2011)

Overcome Stress with Balance: Four Elements that Make Life Easy (2011)

The Science of Smell: How Aromatherapy Relieves Stress (2011)

Short Stories
A Conversation with Death (2012)
(As published in *A Book About Death*)

For the Love of Coffee (2011)

Tiny Nibbles (2012)

Kristina,
When you find yourself
underwater,
Just start kicking

ISBN: 10-1478146672
(paperback)
ISBN: 13-978-1478146674
(ebook)

Printed in the United States of America.

Permissions:
Photography: Micah Reese DejaBlue Photography www.dejabluephoto.com
All Rights Reserved.
Model: Bree Reese www.breereese.com
Design: Allan Sparks www.sparksart.webnode.com
Editing: Brandy Grey
Web Design: Nye Walker www.netnye.com

For more information about special discounts for bulk purchases or to bring
this author to your live event, please visit our website www.msraejones.com

Third Paperback Edition 2013.

Self-published through CreateSpace printing and distribution.

**Names in some of these stories have been changed to protect the innocent,
or... not so innocent.**

For the Dragoman, his ability to save the souls lost in the desert and breathe fire underwater.

An Underwater Map

Acknowledgments	*8*
Note from the Editor	*10*
Preface	*12*
Act I - Splash	**17**
Champagne	19
The Water Monster	25
Enlightenment	49
Secrets, Lies & Firsts	57
War	79
Act II – The Deep	**87**
Jim, Jack, John and Jose...	89
Man-Meat	101
Daywalkers	105
Waves	119
The Light	127
I don't	145
Burn, Baby, Burn	149
Act III – Kiss of the Dragon	**161**
An Affair to Remember	163
Lost	177
The First Hit	187
Murder Creeps from the Cracks	193
Truth Tripping	197
She Speaks	209
The Cliffs	215

Act IV – Conversations & Cannibalism   **223**

    Judge, Jury & Executioner   225

    Gods & Sharks   235

    Crossed Legs & Coffee   241

About the Author   **247**

Acknowledgments:

To those who have forgiven me, as I have forgiven myself. To those with strength, and reflected to me my own. To those who have struggled and fought and lashed out, and the single breath that has saved them. To those that have remained calm in the face of adversary. To those heros in every day life.

Thank you. All my love and gratitude to those who believed in and supported this book. My humble thanks do not do it justice.

To my parents, who I love unconditionally and who, when they read this, I know their heart will break into a million pieces. I know they will wish they knew, I know they will wish they could have done something, I know they will read bits of this and cry and put the book down only to pick it back up again and continue reading. I pushed them, tested them, and was the worst possible daughter (at times) and they still loved me. And, I know that at the end of this story, after all of it, they will be proud. They will know that they did an excellent job, and there will still be love. Through everything, there will be love.

To Peter. I never know what the future holds, but I know that without you, there wouldn't have been one. Thank you for the safe space in your soul in which I live. You have been the Sun in the center of my Universe. Your orbit has effected me deeply and will last until the ends of eternity.

To Kari, I wish I could have been there for you, I wish I could have been the sister that was close, and friendly and loving. I'm sorry I wasn't. But, I am here now, and will be in the future-no matter what. You and me against the world.

To Naomi for the encouragement, Casey for the example of grace and Mikaela for the bright light of hope. To Endi, Jennette and the rest of the dancing ladies, thank you for the foundation of feminine grounding to which held the key for finding my feet. To Jules for the second set of eyes, tough questions and gentle critique. To Micah, for the ability to capture everything I could imagine into an image. To Bree and her daringness to be the face of this journey. To Sparks, for the flawless design, only the Gods should be so lucky. To Nye and making the impossible real in the virtual world and weaving your magic on the web. To Amber and the mirror, showing me the fearlessness and courage it took to finish this. To Eyefleye, for the beautiful sacred safe space and light you hold.

To my editor Brandy, for asking the tough questions. For holding space in your heart for me to work through the tough stuff on my own. For ripping it all apart just to put it delicately back together again. For sharing, smashing and swimming through the bottles of champagne until it was finished.

A Note from the Editor:

It's not uncommon for artists to labor under the assumption that our best ideas, our most powerful work, will come to us on our death bed.

But, even if you have an acute awareness of the impermanent nature of all things -your own mortality included– it is impossible to know what will really come in that moment. And it will come.

What if it was today? Right now.

Rae Jones came to me with this manuscript insisting *she was not really a writer* – this, after releasing nine publications in one year. It was a memoir, and she was as tentative as anyone who told the whole, complete truth in writing might feel.

I read it in one sitting. It was dismantling and wry - but not affected or contrived. Structured in the cacophonous moments we sweep away *if we can* until our chaotic, adrenaline-filled last breath of air, when all things come full circle. This book is not just a collection of transgressions, mistakes and triumphs. In *Breathe*, Rae Jones walks the threshold between the dead and the living.

Immediately, I knew my job as an editor would be to encourage this structure, which provides a beautiful showcase for her words, and to demand four more chapters, at least. Insisting on anything less would have sold her short. For, Rae Jones is very much an artist – and very much a writer.

Artists are brave. When something terrifies or repulses us, we don't stop looking. Even when we flinch. Stomachs churning, palms sweating, heart racing - we get acquainted. In fact, we get as close as possible until finally realizing what needs to be said. To do anything less is to accept a lesser version of ourselves. Better to speak than let silence whittle you down to nothing.

All this takes bravery, honesty, perseverance - and for that I am whole-heartedly proud to be involved in this book, for *Breathe* allows Rae Jones to take us on this journey with her. Furthermore, I eagerly anticipate the work yet to come – whatever moments inspire it.

~Brandy Grey

Preface:

"I want you to paint me a picture." He said.

I was laying in bed for the umpteenth day, depressed and unmotivated by anything in the world. I whined back:

"I have no canvas, I have no brush. The closest I got was finger-painting when I was six."

"Then paint with your words. Tell me a story, and not something ridiculous like flying broomsticks and glittery vampires. But, something real. Something deep. Paint the song of your soul, so I can't help but sing along."

And I did...

.... the words came out like slippery eels of the devil's tongue and the truth lashed out like a worm in an apple. The journey we take together through these words will not be easy. I was not blessed with the gilded tongue of an MFA or PhD, I do not have the glowing tip of Lucifer's charm of Eve, but you will feel him just the same.

"Writing a memoir is like preparing yourself to go to confession," says Frank McCourt, who didn't publish *Angela's Ashes* until he was 66. "You have to examine your conscience," and that entails honesty. "You can't write an effective memoir if you are worried about family and friends looking over your shoulder. Even if the truth hurts, if it is truthful, then there is no other way to present it. At the very least, readers will recognize the courage in that and respect you for it."

These are my memories, and as memories do over years of anguish, they sneak and slide and snake their way around the subconscious. The memories I have are marked by a mental unhingedness, and yet I claim them as my truths. My point of view and my experiences. They belong to me. They lived inside my skin for years, thrashing about inside my house of flesh. Everyone has a unique point of view about events, as each person perceives the world through different eyes.

This is my story about a breath.

Breathing underwater means not much more than getting in over your head... but more than that, it means, getting in over your head and then figuring out how to get out again. Looking at *Hopeless* and saying,

"I know. It's okay. We can figure this out."
...and Pandora winks at you. And sometimes you drown.

Stephen King writes; "Language doesn't always have to wear a tie and lace-up boots... Writing is seduction."

So, get ready to be seduced. Get ready to forget that you are even reading a story at all, but live this life with me. Travel with me. Feel my joy and pain and love and hurt. But before any of that can happen, we must share a moment of intimacy.

You and I are going skinny dipping.

Before we jump into the wettest of wets, we first have to take off all of our clothes. Standing there, naked, covered only in our shame before we even get to the wet part. I'm going to make you stand there and look at me in my shameless glory. I will whisper in your ear with my over-plump black type. My lingerie-clad words and stocking-footed sentences will wrap around your waist. My skin will slither and move around your body until you are wearing a coat of flesh fashioned from my scars. Your breath will quicken with each paragraph, pant with each quip. My apple to your mouth. You will learn the beat and your body will move and dance when the words fail us.

Our private conversation.

Our private moment together.

Just you and me.

Words on paper.

Skin on skin.

This is just brushes and paint, tools and carpentry, words and style, music and dance. But, when we move together, it is magic and telekinesis.

You will be so consumed with the seduction, you will forget that this whole time we have already been underwater and you are holding your breath.

By the end of it, we will be lovers, friends and confidants. You will know my most intimate of secrets and be with me through the raw exposal of my soul.

and... you will breathe with me.

and... for that, I will love you.

ACT I - Splash

We all die.
The goal isn't to live forever,
the goal is to create something that will.

~Chuck Palahniuk

Champagne

"Come quickly, I am tasting the stars!"

~Dom Perignon

A breath was just about a foot away. But trapped between me and the rest of my life was water. A clear, glistening, jeweled liquid, refracting the rays that shown above it.

Water.

Sustaining our little 3rd rock from the sun.
At that moment, it was my mortal enemy.

As each beautiful, life-giving, air-trapped bubble escaped from my lips and nose, I was acutely aware of the shrinking size from one to the next. One by one, smaller and smaller, until the bubbles were no larger than the fizz of champagne.

Champagne.

A celebratory, fizzy, bubbly, dry and sweetly tart liquid that dances on the tongue. Champagne, which heralds good news, announcements and congratulations. New beginnings such as weddings, births and graduations. The sweet-tarty little bubbles encapsulate an initiation, a joy, an elation of life.

And yet, this champagne was snuffing me out.

Bubble by small fizzy bubble.

My chest burning, my heart pounding in my temples, my eyes bulging and my throat swelling up like a water balloon. My brain was starting to sweat and the dull grey-blackness was starting to enter the corners of my vision.

This champagne, these bubbles, this water and the weight of a 200 pound man who was holding me under. There is a second, a split-second when your brain becomes acutely aware of its last moments and everything starts moving faster and slower at the same time. Like the fabric of time and space ferociously ripping open at the seams, and you are cascading down a worm hole. I specifically remember this moment. Aware of not being able to breathe. Desperate, clawing, grasping, pleading and begging to breathe. Time slowing, fabric ripping, the darkness at the edges of my sight slowly advancing on the bright crystalline water.

And just like the fizz of champagne, the bubbles eventually subside no matter how hard you shake it.

It was not by shock, horror, excitement or even holding my breath, which is what one could do, to feel this irrevocable yet memorable experience of not breathing. But to really not be able to breathe.

To drown.

Gasping.

No Air.

There have been many times of not-breathing in my breathing life, but the first, the first is always the one you remember the most. The first is all the emotions of fear and ecstasy rolled into one.

No Air.

The first.

To rage and rage and rage and cry and cry and cry and laugh and love and lick the sky....

with No Air.

But the first time. The first sears your brain like a hot branding iron. It is forever emblazoned in your memory like a bad acid trip. The first dance with the devil, the first kiss on the lips of the Mistress of Mayhem, the first taste of death.

This first taste was given to me by drowning. The cold liquid, like sharp ice crystals, ripping the insides of my lungs.

One word kept rolling, lolling, screaming, crying and dulling my brain. Over and over again.

Air.

Death was seducing my soul. The deafening violence of silence which had me trapped underwater. This combination of thrashing, bubbles, whooshing and my own hollow screams echoing through time and space. The vibrations don't carry as far underwater as they do on land and yet, I would imagine the same sounds in space. An open, empty, hollow and infinite scream.

There was no God there screaming back.

Nothing. Just emptiness. My screaming had found a black hole.

I don't remember exactly how my nose and lips broke the surface of the water. I don't remember what happened as I flailed and frantically grasped at the edge of the pool. But I do remember that first breath. The first mind-numbing, lung-burning, life-saving breath. I remember the instant flood of oxygen to my brain and body and how it combined with endorphins and adrenaline and made me instantly high. Coughing, churning, spitting, cursing and ridiculously, ecstatically, high.

High on everything, and everyone.

On air, on chemicals released into my body, and on life.

High.

My first high.

I was 15 years old when the Mistress of Death uncorked that bottle of Champagne.

The Water Monster

"It's funny how humans can wrap their mind around things and fit them into their own version of reality."

~**Percy,** *The Lightning Thief*

"She really has a talent."

They were talking about me.

"You should really consider having her join the team for the summer."

It was so hot. The concrete deck was burning the bottoms of my feet. The air was still, thick and sweltering, and two men were talking to my mother. Two incredibly handsome, tall, dark, athletic and tanned men were talking about me. ME! What would she say to them as the fiery orb of infinite hotness blazed on us?

"We really can't afford it right now," she said.

WHAT?! My small sun-seared and light-blinded eyes peered up first at her, then back to them. Hopping from foot to foot to escape the fiery death of concrete cooked toes.

"But, you don't understand, she is incredibly talented and could easily go to college on a scholarship with just a few years training. We have just seen what she did and that is really impressive. She out-swam the rest of her class by an entire lap and they were only supposed to go to the wall and come back. The rest of her class is almost twice her age. Please, at least consider it."

I was just 7 years old the summer my parents had enrolled me into the American Red Cross Swim program. An hour a day, so that I could learn how to swim, but probably more important, I could learn how not to drown. These men were not with the Red Cross. They were recruiting me. They saw potential to do more than just *not drown*.

Every year during the summers of the late 80's/early 90's my extended family on my father's side would meet up and we would spend at least a week out camping, skiing, tubing, and rafting at Cove Palisades in Central Oregon.

My paternal grandparents had four children. My father is the oldest, my aunt Jane, then My Uncle Adam, and finally, the youngest Aunt Charlotte.

Aunt Jane is married to a nice man named Rob and together they have four daughters. Aunt Jane and her husband had a very large Sea-Swirl ski-boat, and their daughters would usually bring a few friends with them on this annual trip. The more the merrier.

Uncle Adam is married to a beautiful woman named Lidia. They have two sons and a daughter. They also had a ski-boat. Uncle Adam always had the coolest, newest toys. He introduced us to Kneeboarding (back in the late 80's when it first started becoming popular), and wake-boarding in the early 90's when glorified skateboard decks were just hitting the scene. He was cool, hip, young and wild. He found a secret little bridge over the water and would take all the kids out there to jump off. Wild! Uncle Adam and his wife would usually invite some of their friends who also had ski-boats and kids about the same age.

And, at the time, Aunt Charlotte was in her early 20's, going to college, single with no kids. She would sometimes bring along her friends.

The more the merrier.

It was a beautiful relatively unknown spot back then. A spot in the bullseye of beauty which is the state of Oregon. It is a high desert of towering cliffs which border a marriage of three rivers. The Deschutes, Crooked and Metolious. The watery movement of all three come together in kiss of openness called Lake Billy Chinook. The edges of sight from the water are the glorious Cascade Mountain vistas and basalt spires resting high against the sky. Soaring bald eagles and songs of wildlife echo off of the steep canyon walls. It is hiking trails, water sports and camping against a backdrop of spectacular scenery.

The days were spent swimming, kneeboarding and playing in the sun. At night, the adults would pour drinks - lots of drinks - play jokes on each other. All of the kids would rehearse skits and dramatic plays, which included gymnastic moves, dancing, singing and a lot of bad 7 year old acting. When I say the *adults* and *kids* I mean 10-12 adults, extended family and friends and all their kids (close to 16 or so). The performances were mostly arranged and choreographed by me and my twin cousins who were about the same age.

It was lovely.

In the evenings, my cousins, myself and my sister would act and sing and do mild gymnastics in a choreographed routine. We incorporated frisbees, volleyballs or whatever else we could find as a prop. It kept the kids busy and occupied while the adults were cooking and cleaning up after the day's activities. We would practice and plot and prepare prior to dinner, while Moms and Dads, Grandparents, Aunts and Uncles would park the boats and pour drinks. Once everyone was fed, and the sun was resting lazily against the cliffs, cartwheels and songs and clapped hands would commence before hugs, kisses, teeth-brushing and bedtime. Everyone would shuffle back to their tents.

The next morning at about 5 a.m., it would start all over. At 5 a.m. the water is like glass and the skiing is amazing. The daytime was filled with thoughts of new flips, new songs, new suntans and my Uncle Adam's brand new knee-board. My family loved it. Everyone loved it. It was a beautiful ritual, and a great way for everyone to get together, unwind, spend time with family and take a vacation.

Even as a young girl I never had a problem with swimming, treading water, doggy paddling, holding my breath and floating. I was always comfortable in the water.

A year before the conversation between my mother and those two handsome men on the pool deck, something happened. Something which changed the direction of all of our lives. That day, a year prior, my Uncle Rob loaded up his boat with his wife Jane, my other uncle Adam, my mother and myself to spend a few rounds out on the water on a beautiful sunny afternoon. They all took turns. I wiggled and basked in the sunshine. In my self-made throne on the bow of the boat, I sipped grape soda and had one responsibility... watch the skier. It was great. I was happy. Slathered in sunscreen, holding a bright orange flag, screaming "DOWN" whenever someone was done with their turn.

I could have been out there forever.

Glancing up at my aunt who was happily slalom skiing behind. The water was smooth, the wind was calm and the sun was shining. It was the perfect temperature on a perfect day.

She weaved back and forth, back and forth, and finally waving off and letting go. I hollered loud, "DOWN" and my Uncle Rob quickly swung around to pick her up. I was excited, holding the bright orange flag way up in the air. There were no other boaters around, but I didn't care. I was, oh-so-happy. Secretly planning out the nights performance in my head.

It was a normal, awesome, sunny day. Like so many other days before. The sun was warm but not too hot, the water was cool, but not too cold. The shade of the shore offered the perfect place for an afternoon nap, and the coolers were filled with Capri-Suns, fruit and food of all kinds.

My uncle Adam was sitting in the co-captain chair wrapped in a fuzzy beach towel. He had taken a round before Jane, whipping in and out of the wake on his knees. Turning and slipping and sliding against the wet glass. Trying out new tricks and turns. It was beautiful. A day like so many others we had. By the time we got turned around and pulled up next to my aunt, she was bobbing happily in the chilly water taking off her ski. As she climbed in, my mom had already started putting on her vest. It was the last round before we were going to head back to shore.

My mom jumped in, Adam tossed her ski to her, then her rope and we sat at idle. I was happy, face to the sun, holding the flag up high, listening to the waves lap against the boat. It was a ritual that had played out a hundred times before, just in that one week.

"HIT IT!"

And we were off.

She was beautiful. Weaving in and out of the wake. She looked like Linda Carter. Black hair, blue eyes, tall, thin, athletic, graceful and beautiful. No, not beautiful.

Stunning.

I loved her.

Then all of the sudden... something went wrong and she was down. Not just down, but tripping over the tip of her ski, flipping and flailing through the air, landing like a scorpion face-first in the water with her legs high up snapping over her back and head. Bodies were not meant to do that. That was not graceful, beautiful or right.

It was very wrong.

Uncle Rob was flipping the boat around and driving full throttle back to where her lifeless body lay face down in the water faster than I could even utter a sound.

Faster than I could grab the flag.

Her body was lifeless, unmoving in the water and last I checked, she didn't have gills. I was scared. Rob didn't even slow down when we got close to her. Adam just jumped, no he FLEW off the side of the boat and into the dark water. Like a secret Superman with his towel catching the wind off his back. A superhero who was going to save my mother. He instantly disappeared into the dark water. The water was dark. There were monsters in that water now. Big, scary, hungry, monsters. Monsters that only a 7-year-old could dream up. Monsters that ate the beautiful mothers of the world.

All of the sudden everything was dark and gray. There was no longer bright sunshine, no longer blue skies, no longer water lapping against the boat. Everything was gray, the birds were screeching not singing, the cliffs were looming, the water was dark and foreboding, and the boat was cutting like a knife through it all. The air was deafeningly still.

It was like nature was holding its breath and screaming out loud at the same time. Screaming for her to breathe.

Screaming for her to move.

I held my breath with everything else and waited.

By the time Rob got the boat turned around and slowed down, Adam had carefully turned my mother over so she was floating on her back. She was breathing, but just floating there. Unmoving. Her eyes were blinking, but you could tell she was scared. But there was light. There was life.

My Uncle Adam was treading water holding her head and neck still, and then it was a blur. Lifejackets were thrown in. Jane jumped in. The water was still dark. But there were pinpricks of light. She was alive. She was breathing, but still not moving. The little light bubbles you could barely see in her eyes, then fizzed, like champagne that had been shaken a little too hard. The little light bubbles were fizzing. Growing.

I didn't understand. I had a thousand questions. I could hardly see. I couldn't hear what they were saying. Seconds seemed like minutes, minutes like hours. But she was alive. She battled the evil water monster and was alive!

It took a good 10-15 minutes before any feeling came back in her legs. And we waited. The adults discussed the *what ifs*, and I heard things like, "how do we get her out of the water without moving her", "should we try and figure out how to get her to a hospital?"

I sat. Wide-eyed. Frozen. Not crying, not moving, not flinching, not anything. Just watching her. Watching the light in her eyes. The little light bubbles, the sparkly champagne bubbles. Her eyes were no longer the bright blue I knew, but overcast with grey.

She looked old.

Frail.

Helpless in the water.

It was a little longer before she was in the boat. Carefully, gingerly, they had helped her in until she was laying on the floor. But she was alive. She was moving, and after a while, she could walk. Delicately, but walking.

There was no more skiing that day.

No drinking that night.

No performances or giggling or shouts of laughter. The water monster had sucked the joy out of the vacation. This monster had stolen the joy and carefree spirit of life right from our family. But I didn't care much about thieves, all I cared about was that my mother was alive. I should have cared though, because in the place of joy, this monster had planted a seed of fear.

I don't remember how much longer we stayed before we went home, I just remember going home. Riding in the car with a new passenger called Quietness. A newly acquired fifth member of the family. One who loomed large with a fist of silence.

I remember my mom not feeling well for a long time. I remember, she was never really the same after that day.

There was never that fiery spark in her eyes again. The little light bubbles came back, the blue in her eyes came back, but the river monster had taken something to keep. She was changed. We all were.

Forever.

She was lucky. We didn't find out until almost 25 years later the extent of damage that was done in her neck. She was very, very lucky. It was all from that one split second, from that one terrifying battle with the monster of the water. She won that day, but the memories and fear remained.

So, when these two handsome, tanned, young men pleaded with her on the deck of the pool,

when they said: *"Please consider it."*

I think it was the memory of that day just a year prior that convinced my mom joining the swim team was a good idea. Eventually the memory of that fateful day, the memories of the the annual summer camping and skiing trip just faded into the background. My uncles still go to that spot. Every year they go. For the last 30 years. I have never been back.

But I will.

I will go back and seek revenge on the beast who stole a piece of my mothers soul.

But, that is not the end of the story, it is only the beginning.

On that one fateful day when my mother almost lost her battle with the Water Monster, my battle with water, my search for revenge, a competitive swimming career and a struggle to breathe under-water began.

She said yes to these two handsome men standing under the hot sun, and promptly at 7:30 a.m. the next morning I stood shivering next to a very large pool on very cold concrete. The men didn't look as handsome as they did the day before. They looked tired. They weren't topless, tan and toned like ethereal Greek Gods. They were, instead, covered in heavy parka's, barking splits, take-off times and instructions. Whistling at the swimmers timed ever so carefully to when their cap-covered heads broke the water for a breath.

I stood there... watching... breathless.

It was the first time I saw this finely tuned orchestratic-esque performance. A sliver of the sun was just starting to peek over the desert in the distance. The sky was aflame with pink, blue, purple and orange hues and the air had a slight chill. The desert in the morning always has a slight chill, and by the afternoon it is blazing hot.

The desert is a beautiful place. A beautiful, raw place of abandonment. Open and exposed to the wildest of weather.

It is a place where the Gods disappeared in some ancient time. A place where they left the corpses to dry and turn to dust. They now sit patiently waiting for your flesh to join the ranks. Deadly heat and flying dust carried by 60-mph winds threaten to strip away your skin with the sand it carries on its every exhale.

Death-Dust.

Desert-Breath.

Lightning strikes and thunder rolls and rain comes down leaving steam rising from the asphalt like a mirage. And... it smells of sage.

Sage and freshly cut hay. It smells of clean and fresh and new beginnings. Old made new, death and rebirth. All of it can happen in a 24-hour period.

On that particular pink-tinted, calm, cold, desert morning. These two men were working together, coordinating the timed splashes, the whistles, and the barking all the while running back and forth on the deck. Pointing, waving, looking at the stopwatches and gesturing wildly to the cap-covered swimmers in the pool.

It was now my turn. And into the frigid waters I went, my chance to join the orchestra. My chance to make music, to train and swim and learn.

In the morning, cold water is a shock to the system, but I learned, the faster I moved, the faster I paddled and kicked, the warmer I became. I was a few laps in, almost halfway through my workout one cold summer morning, when... I saw it.

Saw it with my own small, plastic goggle-covered eyes. I had just pulled my shivering body to the edge of the pool after thrashing through the cold waves. While holding on and catching my breath, I saw it. It was the first one I had seen. Ever. And my mind reeled, my body quit shivering and the inquisitive mind of an 8-year-old who had just seen her first tattoo was like that of seeing a unicorn.

It was a small ink stain in the shape of a crown with small letters between the gold spires. It was on the ankle of this tanned Greek God and it left a permanent stain on my brain. Every day I peered at this ankle. Every day I stared at this glorious Unicorn of Ink and God and Tan and Muscle.

It made me feel funny. It made me feel strong. That permanent little ink stain was always there. Every summer, attached to tanned flesh, walking back and forth on the concrete. And every summer, I waited with wanton breath to see it.

It was mine.

My secret.
My unicorn.

One day I will have it. All my own. My precious.

When most kids were off playing, camping, watching TV, laying in the sun. My summers were now filled with unicorns and split times, stroke counts and technique drills, flip turns, breath counts, and endless calculating from meters to yards, seconds to minutes and back again. Math games. Breath games. And Unicorns.

Head down, stroke, stroke, stroke, bubbles, count and breathe. Hold breath, head down frantic-furious-thrashing-stroking-kicking 1, 2, 3, BREATHE. Head down, thrash and kick and scream and scream and scream under water, until there is no breath, and then, hit the wall.

Then gasp and breathe.

Exhausted. Exhilarated.

What is my time?
Was I fast?
Did I win?
Was I the best?

The answers came by the thousands over the endless summers, sleeping in tents next to a pool. Sometimes the difference between a yes or no was a hundredth of a second.

Do you know how fast a hundredth of a second is?

It is faster than the blink of an eye. It is the time it takes for a bolt of lightning to strike. A hundredth of a second is the difference in a swimmers body between elation and heartbreak. Ecstatic jubilation and defeat. The difference between Junior Olympics and just another weekend swim meet in a small town in Eastern Oregon. A hundredth of a second. It was the difference between a five-year full-ride scholarship and Olympic Training facilities in Colorado Springs, to a community college and a good healthy life-long exercise program.

Hundredths of seconds.

My life was dictated every summer, fall and eventually winter by hundredths of seconds. For every jubilant YES, there were hundreds of heartbreaking no's.

By the time I entered high school I had the summer routine down. A few years earlier those walking, tanned, Greek Gods on the deck had decided I needed to move up and train with the older, and sometimes MUCH older swimmers. Practices now began at 6:00 a.m. I would now watch the sun come up every morning in the desert through my small, sleep-coated and fog-resistant plastic goggles.

> 6:00 a.m. - 7:30 a.m. Practice
> 7:30 a.m. - 8:30 a.m. Breakfast/Rest
> 8:30 a.m. - 11:30 a.m. Teach
> *American Red Cross Swim Classes*
> (things coming full circle by this point.)

11:30 a.m. - 1:00 p.m. Lunch/Rest
1:00 p.m. - 4:00 p.m. Lifeguarding
4:00 p.m. - 5:30 p.m. Swim Team Practice
5:30 p.m. - 6:00 p.m. Dinner/Rest
6:00 p.m. - 8:00 p.m. Lifeguarding

Then go home, eat, sleep, wake-up, lather, rinse and repeat. The cold mornings would turn into scolding hot afternoons and into dusty evenings next to a chlorine-soaked pool, day after day. These were the days of the super-structured, super-summer for a super-swimmer. My skin smelled of bleach, my breath cycled with stroke counts and my skin was as dark and rough as a coconut.

The moments of glorious rest were filled with the obligatory re-application of waterproof sunscreen, drinking as much water/gatorade/juice/liquid as possible, snacking on whatever little horde of food was left in your locker and trying to get a few minutes of shut-eye on a threadbare couch sulking in the corner of the office. Usually the office was so busy with other 'guards and kids and music and announcements, that much resting didn't happen there. It happened around the corner of the building nestled inside a horseshoe shaped out-cut. In the center was a huge grandfather oak tree. Tall and strong, with large green leaves winking at you between the harsh summer sun standing on hard, dusty, dirt-fed yellow grass.

Grandfather Oak, presiding over the pool.
The Pharaoh in the desert.

The glorious resting times when I could sneak away.

I could easily set an internal alarm clock to walk back in the office a few minutes before my next shift. I cherished the times I could lay on the cool ground and trace the veiny leaves with my fingertips. Grandfather Oak was magical and fulfilling, calm and serene in a summer filled with chlorine, split-times and sunshine.

Even after summer ended and the school year began, I would continue the 6 a.m. practices. Even after the school budget dictated that there would be no more cleaning done to the pool, I would still continue. Even when the calendar clicked closer to Halloween than Labor Day,
I was swimming with water skippers and muck locked behind a chain-link fence. It was quite an adjustment for a 14-year-old freshman in a small town.

"Please, please let us out of the pool. I'm freezing."

I could hear the older 16-year-old purple-lipped girls from the lane next to me begging to be let out of practice. On that particular day, it was 6:30 a.m., and I was just finishing an 800 meter warm-up on a frigid October morning.

October in the desert is full of Indian summers, shadowy figures and light dancers. It is full of hauntings and autumn leaves. It is the marriage and synastry of hot summer days and cold nights. It is the smell of death and summer dust being burned away with the fields.

Plump harvest, gleaming sharp knives brandished for slaughter, and dry lightning. Watermelons and warm rain. It is glistening bruised sunsets and florescent pink-orange dawn. Back and forth, waves of an oceanic desert.

<u>October was a time of orbits.</u>

That morning, ominous black clouds were on the horizon and it was just starting to rain in the cold late October way. By afternoon it would be sticky and hot, but right now, it is downright chilly.

The coach scowled at the girls who had stopped and this was all the motivation I needed. I took a look at the exchange and didn't want to listen to the arguments, the begging and the eventual relinquishment of the coach.
I knew they didn't like the icky algae sticking to their bodies. I knew they wanted the extra time to shower and primp and blow dry their hair. Extra time to paint their faces in the only way sophomore girls can, like a crayola factory gang-banged on their flesh.

The rain was pelting down like stinging needles when my arms and head moved out of the water. But funny thing about water, it insulates, it protects, and in the desert of a 14-year-old girl, the storms are silent. I was safe from everything as long as I kept my head under the surface keeping my new family member "Quiet" safely with me. The practice would only last until 7:30 a.m. Classes starting at 7:50 a.m. It was only about an hour away and 2.5 more miles of swimming, 4,000 meters.

I could make it. Only 75 minutes left. Math games, breath counts, meters and seconds.

It wasn't that cold as long as I kept moving.

After just a short time of this schedule, my life existed underwater and no one could beat me in the pool. No one. I was tall, tan, thin, strong and quite possibly in the best shape of my life. I was a God in the water. Not a mermaid, not a fish, I was an All-Mighty, All-Powerful GOD. I had joined the Greeks. I had mastered the pool. I was the Queen of my own domain. I could hold my breath for the better part of three minutes, easily. It was my home, the place where I felt safe, where I knew how things moved and how long life took when under the surface. I didn't have to speak to anyone. My body, the water, and time was my landscape. Quietness ruled.

I held records, I had numerous articles and interviews already published in the local and high school newspapers, and although I wasn't a popular girl in school, I was infamous. Infamous and training to take on the River Monster. Training to seek revenge on the demon who stole happiness from our family and replaced it with an imbalance of fear and quietness. And everything was going along swimmingly (so they say).

Until...

That one day. That one day when that one guy panicked. That one day in the summer when the sun was hot and the pool was cold and I was lifeguarding and he went in a little too deep.

That one day I blew my whistle, loud. Shockingly, piercingly, loud. And everyone looked. Everyone stopped. And then, I jumped in after him. It was that one day, that one moment, when time stopped, there was no breath. There was no air. For over four and a half minutes, there was not one single ounce of air, and no sound, just the sound of bubbles.

Just champagne. Small fizzy little bubbles expelling from my nose.

Congratulations,
You lose.

Congratulations,
There is no air left.

Congratulations, you are not a mermaid or a fish or a Greek God. You will not seek out the River Monster, no, the River Monster has come for you .... and... he brought the Mistress of Death to your door. Oh yes, the Mistress of Death is now kissing you on the lips. She has your number. She is popping the cork on a bottle of Champagne and celebrating. She knows your name and calls for you like a siren from the deep fabric of space.

Seducing you.

You are hers. Forever.

Some have asked me, "what is it like to drown?" and all I can say is, *everyone drowns in something a little bit different* and I tell them...

I tell them to imagine. I tell them to take a deep breath. Then I tell them...

You have plunged through the tension of the surface into cold water. Taking a big breath and a quick glance at the sun before the cold of the water shocks your skin. Then, as time passes while you are still holding your breath under the surface, you start your struggle, your lungs start burning, hotter and hotter and hotter. They start screaming and slashing like a B-List Horror Movie Actress for you to breathe. You fight harder for the surface, squeezing your eyes tighter, defying your basic bodily need, and you hold your breath a little more. Then, you gulp and swallow the air in your mouth, desperately trying to recycle the air already living there. Swallowing, drinking, anything. You gulp again with your lips tightly pressed together. Until you just can't take one more second... you are getting dizzy and disoriented, and you aren't even sure which way is up, other than your automatic clawing at it.

Then.... and only then, you part your lips and sip, trying to sip the oxygen off the hydrogen particles. You are desperate. Your brain has abandoned all logical thinking.

Then... you choke. Your gag reflex takes over and you gasp... Gasp in all the water. Your eyes bulge as your lungs over-expand and find no release against the heaviness of blue. The color seen in your eyes fades to grey and in an instant you are walking a red carpet with lights flashing. Then, it is darkness. Blackness. A silent velvet blanket wrapped tightly around you.

Then.

It is calm. Pure stillness

Then...

Then... by some miraculous power, some thing, some one, or the black hole itself spitting you out and screaming back, you breathe. Your head is above water and there is life. Again. Chaos.

Congratulations, you just cheated.

... and the Mistress of Death does not ever like to be cheated.

Enlightenment

"Knowing others is wisdom.
Knowing yourself is Enlightenment"

~Lao Tzu

When you get high on ecstasy for the first time it is unlike anything you have ever experienced. It is the best, greatest, most colorful, most heart opening and awe-inspiring event ever. It is filled with new feelings, new responses from your body you never thought possible, from the same stimuli you have always received. Memories are relived with this new intensity, passion is felt as a deeper experience, deeper connection, more breath, more love, light, beauty, more of everything. The Universe itself exists at the tip of your finger. And all you want to do is dance. Dance with the colors and the people and the tastes and textures and smells. Dance and dance and dance until your feet are nothing more than bloody, stubby, stumps shoved into shoes.

Then, every time after that first time, you are always chasing that moment. Begging for that peak that was as good as the first, it is good, make no mistake, but it is never enough. Never far enough, just not quite there. But, it is still good.

... or so I have heard....

I could only compare it to what it is like to kiss the Mistress of Death. The first taste is ecstatic. The first taste commands respect. But not just the attitude of respect, it commands respect at a cellular level, calling attention to the very core and essence of self. You see, this Mistress of Death speaks to a part of you that nothing else touches. The part that is hidden and soft and vulnerable. The mistress seduces herself past your walls and blocks and sarcasm and snark and speaks to your soul.

And guess what.....

Your soul responds. It responds in a way that is almost unworldly. Your soul desires this Mistress, and eventually your soul will dance with this Mistress. One day. All of it, everything, is exactly like Ecstasy. Your soul knows the darkness of death intimately and desires to dance and dance and dance again. And you do. Because you know the dance, you know the steps, and the music calls.

It is impossible to have a conversation about life, without talking about death. Yet, in this discussion of death, one is deeply reminded of their own mortality. When the reminder of mortality happens, the deeper questions of life begin to emerge. Fear begins to emerge. The meaning of existence and the questions of life after death are born.

They say; and for the record, I have no idea who *they* are, but will continue to refer to *them* like some faceless-nameless-know-it-all-collection-of-people like God, but different. *THEY* say, one of the ways in which to reach enlightenment is to be aware of every single breath you take in.

Breath.

Air.

God.

Ecstasy.

Freedom.

And you breathe, you try, but ...

God is a long way away from the Mistress of Death.
God is a long way away when you are high on ecstasy.
God is a long way away when years upon endless years are riddled with night-terrors, insomnia and anxiety.

God is really not the first person you think of when you are standing behind a customer service counter and someone comes up to ask a simple question and you are hit with a panic attack, instantly covered in sweat, shaking, heart pounding and looking for the nearest garbage can to puke into.

God doesn't feel any closer when you are all alone in a small one bedroom apartment for days and days on end because of the downright fear of opening the door and being around other people.

God does not exist under water, and I can tell you definitively, I never met God when I kissed the Mistress of Death.

This is a very difficult thing for me to say. God does not exist in these places. It is difficult because coming from a culture and family where I was definitely of the white-bread-protestant-anglo-saxon variety, it is blasphemous. But I guess even in blasphemy, there is truth. The truth for me is that in all my time of parental-forced Sunday School, I could not swallow the one big pill of Jesus Christ being the one and only path to God.

So, with that, by definition, I guess I am not a Christian.

My God is much simpler. It is not something external, my life is not something I need to be saved from.

My God is not a knight on a white horse or a magical Santa Claus in the sky. It doesn't abandon. It doesn't whisper.

My God lives inside, as a strange blended version of Universal Life Force, Energy, Zeus, Vishnu, Thor, the Light, the Higher Power, Jehova, Allah and Goddess-self, Mother Earth type.

But, yet, I struggle.

Struggle with belief and reconciling all of these thoughts and doubts and feelings swimming around, drowning in doubt.

This does not help in a moment of panic.

And THEY say, in those moments, the moments you are panicky and desperate and doubting and losing focus, THEY say, it is because you aren't breathing. THEY say it is because you aren't connected to God or the Universe or some other Bodhisattva-like Nirvana. Some ecstatic feeling in merging with everything.

The peace. The calm.

The eye in the storm of life.

They say; The more you focus on your breath, the more you meditate, the more you let go of everything else, everything else which clutters up your mind, making it race and race and race around in circles like an OCD Nascar race, the more you will feel-see-touch-hear-experience this enlightenment

So, I gave up ecstasy. Gave up booze and men and drugs and sought ecstasy through enlightenment. Ecstasy through Enlightenment. Chased some ecstatic celebration and merging with the Universe in a natural, meditative, unassisted way.

Enlightenment.

So they say.

With Breath.

It all happened in a clarifying moment of piss and puke. Clarifying in a way a bender can make you clear. Not a *dark night of the soul*, no big *call for a savior*, or reborning sense of transformation. But clear in the way the first gasp of air feels like after drowning in prescription bottles and vodka flasks.

Yet, as clear as I got, I could never give up the ecstasy that the Mistress of Death brought to me. I could never give up the water. It was strange, I knew God-Enlightenment-Ecstasy-Whatever-you-call-it, didn't exist underwater and but I still wanted to believe, I wanted to believe in something. I wanted to believe that something in this physical world could bring to me the highs that the dance with Mistress of Death had brought. I wanted to believe in life.

Ecstatic.

Rolling.

Glorious.

Life.

They promised this. *They* promised empowerment. *They* promised enlightenment. *They* promised the peace and love and nirvana-like experience in which I thought I was missing. If I studied hard, practiced what was being preached and took every class I could, I could have it.

I wanted it.

I needed it.

I craved to suck all of the empowerments and energy as possible out of this *secret esoteric society* that I was initiated into as possible. It was as addicting as the relationship between a drunk and a bottle. Only it was rooms of dry drunks replacing obsessive emotional addictions with empowerment.

In every belly, there is acid to digest the delicious. Even in the belly of the beast that is empowerment.

Energy, Initiations, Art and Gods. The contemplation of these few things for those few years affected me deeply and changed my life.

I learned that no matter how enlightened or empowered, everyone is still deeply flawed. Everyone is still fighting their own demons, and sometimes those fights spill out onto the street. I learned that there are a lot of different places you can receive back-up during a blood-soaked street fight, and sometimes *light-workers* are scared of the dark and won't meet you for those rat-infested midnight brawls. When that shift in perspective happened, it was life-altering. It is almost like seeing the Wizard behind the curtain.

After that, I could no longer believe in the fairy tales.

Secrets, Lies and Firsts.

"Everybody has a secret world inside of them.
All of the people of the world, I mean everybody. No
matter how dull and boring they are on the outside,
inside them they've all got unimaginable, magnificent,
wonderful, stupid, amazing worlds. Not just one world.
Hundreds of them.
Thousands maybe."

~Neil Gaiman

I wish I could say the first time was gentle, beautiful and perfect. I wish I could say it was everything I had hoped it would be, seen in the movies, read about in books and heard about from friends.

But it wasn't.

There were no candles, no romance, no dinner, no promises, no nothing. In fact, there was nothing nice, soft or perfect about the experience. It was raw, bloody, violent and …

...soul-less.

Vampiric almost. Predatory in its very essence. I drowned again that day. Choking, sputtering, coughing and drowning in my own slippery, coppery tasting blood. Vampiric. Blood.

I was 15-years-old, and it was just a few short months after I cheated the Mistress of Death for the first time. She had come back.

Come back with a vengeance.

Seeking restitution.

Back to claim what had been stolen from her.

My life.

It started simply enough. Come over after lunch, watch the football game for a bit, chat about the current high school drama, go home, get ready, go to the homecoming dance that night. Simple.

The day before, on Friday, there was an excited static buzz in the air of the local High School. The *girl-friends* cackled about their dresses, their shoes, the flowers, their hair, making plans to get ready together before the dance. They are prancing glittery ponies. They gossip about which one of their boyfriends will be crowned Homecoming King at the game.

They chatter about the rumor that the English teacher is having an affair with the copy assistant. And they make snide comments about everything which isn't up to their glittery standard. It could have been a scene stolen directly from the movie *Clueless*. The boys could give a shit about the dance. They wanted the Friday night game. They wanted the after-party, and they all hoped to score with their respective prancing pony.

Instead.... on Saturday, something else entirely, happened. Something dark and cruel and completely necessary. It was a glorious orbital October day. The smell of crisp leaves, crinkling and dancing down the street with the breeze. It is football season, high school dances and dress-up. Faces of created and hollowed out ghouls await with heavy anticipation of dusk and the lighting of a fire in their bellies to beacon forth those masked and caped in nearly a week. The small town is abuzz, the local high school hosts a homecoming dance tonight. Flower shops are busy with corsage's, boutonnieres, bouquets and balloons. Car washes are packed with young boys taking their dad's car to get washed before the prince and his chariot will pick up his princess of the night. Last night the football team lost the homecoming game, but that's nothing new to this small town of farm-boys and 4-H'ers. They haven't won a single game in three years. No matter, there was still plenty of screaming and excitement when the Homecoming court was announced at half-time. A ritual repeated thousands of times across the country, to the same, excited screams.

I don't remember much of that particular Saturday, but I do remember flashes. Adrenaline and horror-soaked flashes. Flashes like a dream you had and bits and pieces come back to you in the most inappropriate of places. Only the dream isn't really a dream, it's more like a nightmare, and it's not really a dream because it is real.

I remember, the blood. Like some horrific ritual sacrifice, there was a lot of blood. Not blood which welcomes womanhood and maturity, but blood from a dark, evil place. Unnatural blood. An initiation into darkness with blood. I remember his eyes. Flashing and aflame with evil. Every micro-second of remembering, feels a lot like …

… re-living.

I remember and relive the coppery, slippery, warm liquid as it is coagulating and sliding down my squeezed throat. Sending an infinite amount of *very wrong* signals to my brain. Every rational thought and cellular sense firing, knowing instinctively that something is wrong. Very very wrong. Yet, in that moment, the apex of gurgling, of esophagus-crushed, warm, drowning, there was something so peaceful. While foreign hands were wrapped tightly around my neck, and knees and body weight and elbows were crushing upon my chest. While the ripping and tearing and most grotesque sounds of the human body were happening, lights appeared.

Bright, flashing, like I was famous, beautiful and walking down a red carpet. These tiny flash bulbs were popping, leaving bright, blinding, lights in their wake, I was entranced by those lights, invited by the glow. The bright followed intensely by patches of darkness. The darkness was soothing. The darkness was welcoming. I followed the lights into the darkness. The darkness which grew and grew and grew until it was all that was left. Warm, complete, silent blackness. A soft, velvety blackness with no pain, no fear, no sound and no gravity. A vampire in a coffin, and this dark rite was complete. A warm, silent, completely black, encompassing blanket ... of death. Seduced, bitten, and finally I was bore in the dark.

Floating free.

Again.

High.

Again.

Studies say that every one in four women are the victims of sexual assault. I believe that number to be much, much higher. Because, I never reported anything. I never told anyone. It was my first secret. A secret I kept for many, many years. Too many years. With this secret, I created a world inside myself and locked myself up in it. The walls were built of shadowed lies, the windows of firsts, and this dark tower I built is where I held my soul hostage. Joy locked like a prisoner in the Tower of London.

Locked away.

For years.

Before that day, I had never so much as kissed a boy, and months later, when I finally did... it was hollow. The kissing and fondling and fucking was hollow for years.

Vampires are hollow creatures. Eternally empty.

There was a first of many things that happened that fateful day. It was the first dance I had ever been asked to, it was the first time I could stay out past 10 p.m., and it was the first day I ever looked my folks straight in the eye and lied.

Lied.

It was all lies...

… and all fear.

As a 15-year-old girl, you are afraid of a lot of things. But, that instance, I was afraid of things that weren't even real. I was afraid someone would find out at school and I would be *that girl*. That racy, slutty girl. *That girl* who wanted it anyway, but instead it was *that girl* who got the Homecoming King arrested. *That girl* who ruined his chance for a scholarship, or a life, or a career, or a normal family.

I was afraid of being branded. Afraid no one would believe me. I was afraid of the repercussions from friends, neighbors and other students if I said anything. Afraid of the judgement, shame and brutal rumors that would swirl around my family's reputation.

I couldn't do that to them.

I was afraid that if word got out, it would ruin my father. My dad is a gentle soul with a tender heart and I was afraid that if I told him he would feel like it was all his fault, like he failed in some way. I was afraid he would rage or cry all at the same time. I was afraid he would hunt this boy down with a shotgun and end up in jail (or worse). I was afraid his heart would break until it stopped beating. I was afraid of being a disappointment, and afraid of not being a good role model for my younger sister. I was afraid of everything. Shockingly, traumatically, afraid.

Sometimes bad thing happen to good people. And sometimes, it happens to make them stronger.

I know that now.

But, at 15-years-old, how do you speak those sentences to the people you love? How do you speak woman words with girl lips? How do you express the expressionless. . .

That question continues to haunt me every October like a ghost in the attic of my soul.

Years later, after telling the hard facts from lover to friend, I feel as though in those moments of conversation, I somehow changed in their eyes. I was treated differently. Looked at differently. Interacted with differently. Further way almost, like I was dirty or contagious. Like the things that happened to me could crawl out of my skin and taint them. Like my experience would somehow attack them, and they wanted to be far away from it.

Instinctively I knew those reactions would happen, even at 15, and the truth was, I didn't want to change. I wanted to pretend nothing happened and go on my merry little happy sheltered small town life. I wanted to live the Ever After. I wanted to believe in the fairytale. But... the changes happened anyway, on the inside. It soul shattered, and although the world didn't change around me, the lens I looked out did.

And, that particular day, I was a scared shaking 15-year-old girl that grew up way too fast. Had an experience that 15-year-old girls should not have. And I didn't want to have to talk about the girl things that girls don't want to talk about. I was scared.

But, there was more.

That day, someone accidentally walked in and got an eye-full of the Mistress of Death seducing me. Someone else who saw her Homecoming King puppet. I was scared because this Mistress of Death was determined to take a soul. I was scared, because... She did. Three days later.

It wasn't mine...
It was his.

This unsuspecting soul who walked into the wrong room at the wrong time and looked into the terror-filled eyes of the wrong girl, paid the ultimate price. I don't know what exactly he saw. I didn't even know he was in the house at the time. I just remember the split second in the midst of the chaotic screaming, punching, bright lights and struggle there was a noise at the door. I remember being held down and desperately trying to get up and look to see who it was, trying to scream for help, when I saw the 6'2" linebacker-sized noise at the door. He only stood there for a brief moment, locking eyes with me for a split second. A split second I will never, ever, ever, forget. Before running out of the room and getting into his truck and leaving. He was not helping. He was LEAVING. I could hear the driver's side door slam on his pickup and hear the engine roar to life. I could hear the last bit of Pandora's "Hope" leave with the smoke and squeal of his tires. I can't say what he was thinking or feeling at that moment. Although, I can only assume, that like me, all he wanted to do was run away from the horror. But, it didn't take long. Not long at all for the Mistress of Death, like some possessed parasite in his mind, to see him and take him for her own. And when the news broke in the small town that he had committed suicide, I thought I knew why. And... I was scared. In my 15-year-old brain, I was scared beyond belief. Scared that if I told anyone, they would end up just like him. I was scared for my family, my friends and myself.

It took me years and years and years to come to that conclusion that this boys death wasn't my fault. Years of pain and frustration and guilt and agony and fear and regret. Years of stress and anxiety and obsessive-compulsive controlling behavior. All these secrets locked up and swimming inside my soul, nipping like little piranas on my sanity. Secrets I kept in silence. Secrets that I thought would protect the people I loved. Secrets that instead, kept me bound. Secrets kept me hostage. Secrets made me crazy.

I lied.

Everything was fine.

Everything. Was. Fine.

Even though, that day, I woke up in a pool of blood, in a deserted dusty field of overgrown weeds to the commanding, body-shaking roar and whistle of a train just inches away from my flesh.

Even though the pain was so intense I felt like my skin was ripping apart at the seams. Even though my bones felt like shattered glass. Even though... even though....

Even. Though.

I walked home. I took a shower. I put on make-up. I got ready for the dance. Put on my coat of thick skin and got ready for the performance of my life.
And everything was fine.

I went to the homecoming dance that night. *It was fine....* Like a perfect student, daughter, sister, athlete and friend was fine. I did everything I was supposed to do *finely* under the cover of carefully applied make-up, dissociation and searing white hot pain. I did everything perfectly. I protected everyone perfectly. By distancing, by disassociating, by lying.

I lied to everyone and everything.

For the first time.

Lies.

All of it was one, great, big lie.

And then... forgotten time happened. Forgotten time is that knowing of time passing, knowing I went to school and did all the things I was supposed to do, but like some walking zombie. I was just a hardened empty shell with a smiling face. Forgotten was the joy-filled memories of childhood. Happiness and elation wiped from some etherial memory.

The time is lost in space dust.

I remember ending up in the hospital. I remember my mother talking to the doctor. I remember the look of disappointment on their faces, and I remember them asking me questions. But reaching inside for a truthful response was like reaching into an empty room. I would have to cross that long room first before I could reach my hand out and touch the answer. The lies were so much closer, and I could keep the door to that room closed. So, I lied. The first time I was asked what happened down there - I lied. The first time I was told that an infection left untreated had spread inside my body and into my organs - I lied. I lied and lied and lied. I lied to myself. I lied to my parents, and over the years I lied to doctors and nurses and teachers and anyone and everyone who was within earshot. When reality hit, I tried to lie myself out of it. Tried to slice my flesh out of the reality of where I was. I felt like the grapes in the bottom of the barrel, smashed by oversized Italian feet. Wincing as the skin broke and oozed intoxicating liquid to be enjoyed by everyone at the party. But, the slashing of wrists in the bathroom made a terrible mess and in some sane sense of reality, I was scared I would get blood on the carpet.

Years later, my feet in stirrups and all alone with no one but a nice woman at Planned Parenthood and my own shadows locked behind an exam room door. She said:

"You have severe damage. There is so much scar tissue you will never be able to have children."

And, I lied. For the first time. The biggest lie I told. The biggest lie I repeated to myself for years and years and years.

"Good. I don't want them."

I had no idea what the truth was anymore.

Dear Mistress, I guess you did win that day. In spades.

When a child is born, they are not given a manual on how to behave. Most parents do not take classes and certainly aren't imparted instant knowledge on how to raise a child. Things that happen in a delivery room do not change anything. Nothing is ever perfect. Not that day, nor any day after. AND... and, you just work your way through it. Firsts are: messy, rude, ill-timed, dirty, un-called-for, rough around the edges and deliciously, disastrously, perfectly the first.

Like me. I was the first-born child. I was also the first-born grandchild (on my father's side), so that's a lot of first-ing going on in one day and every day since.

Some of my first memories as a young child were that of visiting my grandparents. As the first grandchild, there was the deep bond and connection. My grandmother would spend hours putting my hair in curlers, brushing it out and pinning it up. We would slather Oil of Olay on our faces and make sandwiches with tea while we watched *Wonder Woman* and *As the World Turns*. We played *Memory*. My memories came back with thoughts of her. Memory, playing with those stupid cards, over and over and over again. She taught me how to play cribbage, poker and blackjack. She kept a squeaky cookie drawer and hanging on the walls of the kitchen was her collection of antique silver spoons and a painted wooden plaque I would sing to-

Rich man, poor man, beggar man, thief, doctor, lawyer, merchant, chief, tinker, tailor, cowboy sailor.

She smelled of pink lotion and deep perfume, with candy apple red lips, pin curls and knee-high stockings. And... and her goddamn purple housecoat. She believed in the possibility that I could be Wonder Woman herself. A belief I treasured until I saw for my own eyes, my real-life Wonder Woman do the skiing-scorpion trick. By then, my obsession turned to the Bionic Woman. Re-runs were on TV, and I wanted to believe them when they said:

We will rebuild her.

But, my grandmother, she was always there. Explaining the tough answers to questions I didn't want to ask. She was my breath, and my first death. She was the first to die with my secrets, and she was the first dead body I ever saw.

In October.

I was 20-years-old. She was my first death personified in external despair.

After numerous other funerals and memorial services of friends and relatives, I would always slip out of line before everyone was expected to parade in front of the casket to give their last respects. I never wanted to look at the body. I never wanted to see the formaldehyde flesh laying there on display in pressed satin fluff.

Yet, it was only a day or two after she died, and a few days before the cremation and memorial service. I remember walking into the funeral home. I remember being escorted down a hallway. There were curtains and doors and a strange pungent odor of sadness, chemicals and over-ripe flowers. I couldn't distinguish whether I was smelling the clutching sound of misery, or hearing the cloying odor of death. The scent of decay was sweet and clasping, groping for life with hunger both greedy and hateful.

A perfect Mistress.

Then, hidden behind a door to the right, it opened, and there she was. Laying on a table in her purple housecoat and slippers. She looked as though she could have just stood up from the table and come home with me. Come home and put curlers in my hair. Come home and watched *Wonder Woman*. Come home and play blackjack for pennies and talk about traveling. She was so pretty, her delicate face, fine nose, red lips and chin held up like an ancient queen. Her hair in soft curls, ringlets framing her face. Her cheeks with a slight rosy gleam, and she must have just done her hair. The silvery blackness a perfect juxtaposition for the creamy skin it framed. She must have been getting ready for the day. She looked like she was ready to go. I wanted to reach out and touch her. Touch her one last time. Touch her and take her with me.

But, I didn't. I should have. But, I didn't.

She didn't move.

I didn't move.

She didn't blink, I didn't blink. It was a stand-off.

Death was more un-real than frightening.

I didn't cry. I just looked. I looked for something, anything, but I never took my eyes off her. She didn't smell dead. She smelled of pink and red and purple, elegance and hollowness. I don't know how long I stood there, and I don't even remember leaving. I just remember telling the rest of the family I had to go, then getting in my car and driving 300 miles away. No memorial service for me. I went far far away. Far away and deep inside. My last hope, my personal lifeguard, my lifelong confidant was now gone, and I was instantly lost. Wanting to believe it was just some bad dream. Wanting to believe that it was all a lie.

She died in October.

Even today, over 10 years later, I find myself wanting to pick up the phone and call her. There is so much stuff we need to talk about. Years and years worth of stuff. I miss her.

That is not a lie.

The only way I have been able to get through it is to pretend that she is still alive, but out traveling (also pretending that this is a time we live in with no cell phones, no Facebook, no instant access to everything-ness, which is getting harder and harder to do), Or, pretend she never existed. Trying to do both is getting to be damn near impossible because her death wasn't a lie. It was a first, and I miss her more than words can adequately describe.

I don't understand this word *GRIEF*, I cannot process the emotion and have tried to leave it like an abandoned banana peel on the side of the freeway. No amount of anything speeds up this *grief* thing. It is on its own schedule and only moves around you when you aren't looking. Like some horrible life-game of red-light, green-light.

So, we perform. We grieve in the silence of night, under the cover of darkness, shrouded by our secrets. We keep our performances in the daylight, under the bright theater lights of the sun. Paint our faces with smiles and appreciation while our heart breaks in silence in our chest. We stand on the stage of ourselves to sing and dance the performance of our lives. We act. We attempt to control or guide the impression we are making through changing, fixing or manipulating the setting, our appearance or our manner. Our actions are dictated by the audience and their instant cheers or jeers in front of us.

Acceptance or Rejection.

And we perform. We choose our props. We adjust to different settings. We splash into the water, treading on the surface silently suffering. It is the perfect performance of never having to worry about holding your breath for long. Until you realize you are in the deep end. The deep end is where you forget. You become the method actor and live your performance. You commit fully to the character and in that, you forget your truest nature.

You forget who you are. Just a speck in the dust-bin of memory. Creating and re-creating characters. Living. Lying. Sometimes for the *first* time.

Again.

First, first, first. The first to bring joy and heartbreak, expectations and responsibilities, stress and anxiety, fear and loathing, addictions and... and... unconditional love.

I remember clearly some of the other firsts in my life.

My first tattoo: much to the chagrin of my parents. I drew it myself, and it is beautiful. It keeps my secrets in it's shadows.

My first drink: sitting on concrete steps at dusk with my dad in front of a tiny yellow house.

My first car wreck: at fourteen riding in a borrowed car in a city 300 miles from home.

My first motorcycle, cigarette and leather jacket.

My first job, marriage and divorce.

My first college degree. The first time I got high, the first time I got pierced, and the first time I fell in love. And my first kiss which was, poignantly, AFTER the first time I tasted my own blood.

My own blood. My own vampiric initiation, my blood-lust ritualistic rite of passage. Passionate, violent, brutal and sexual. It was the splash-down into an ocean of my own being-ness releasing my inner predator, leaving it to swim around inside my flesh. A Vampiric initiation which changed the way the blood flows in my body. It has never been *normal*. My blood sacrifices have always had a few hiccups.

Firsts are a bit like initiations of sorts, seared into your mind. Branded into your brain. A first, whether it be good, bad or indifferent, is a first. Once you get done with doing something for the first time, you look back and think.... *Well, I could have done that better*. And then you choose to either do it again and do it better, or don't. It is a completely personal decision and perhaps it is those decisions which shape our lives. It is that instant decision we make following something new of whether or not we want to do it again, and perhaps do it a little bit better. Give it just a little bit more effort, a little bit more preparation, or just a Little. Bit. More. Of Everything.

A recent friend once told me, "I always try something twice, because I could have been wrong the first time." Touche' my friend, touche'. Yet, sometimes life doesn't give you second chances, and you just have to learn to live with being the first.

On that particular day, the most poignant of my firsts, I didn't transform into a lying, secretive, vampiric beast in an instant. But, I felt something shatter inside. Like a precious crystal goblet which was held by silken heart strings and trust, went tumbling and sailing through the air until it fractured into a million fucking little pieces against a granite hearth. It was a deadly equation of internal fractured mind-sharpened shards, death, lies and time. And in that deadly cocoon of a cocktail, I transformed.

The Mistress of Death infected my brain. She moved into my soul and set up house.

Holding these secrets is like holding your breath. It is a lonely place, breathing only on the inside. Aching for it to get out, like an ice-cream headache all over your body. Yet, the insides smashed and glued back together over time like a mosaic of the mind with crigs and cracks and ghosts moving in the spaces between. It is hard to hold the emptiness alone, in a cruel alternate universe.

I spent a lot of time alone under water. Alone was something I was comfortable with, accustomed to being. My old friend Quietness was comforting. I lived alone, walked alone, swam alone, worked alone and loved being in this alone place. Cold and untouchable on the outside and yet on the inside, everything was warm, quiet and wet. Like being underwater.

Trauma changes the brain. The hippocampus, the narrative memory, until all sense of time and space are gone. Your body and emotions and subconscious take over.

You re-live rather than re-member.

A Kamaloca, an evil enchantment of a fairytale, your own personal hell. Maleficent. Malice Magnificent. Relentless, like the tumbling waves of the ocean just wishing for the pounding to stop for a moment. Wishing the waves calm to catch your breath.

But they don't, and you don't, and you hold it. It is then, and only then, my transformation into a vampire was complete. And guess what? Vampires are born in the dark, don't need to breathe underwater and they definitely don't sparkle.

War

"Whatever we do, we are communicating and interacting all the time; rapport is a tool that gives instant access to other minds."

~ The Book of Half-Truth

"Warfare is simply learning everything about your target enemy, their beliefs, likes, dislikes, strengths, weaknesses, and vulnerabilities.
Once you know what motivates your target, you are ready to being psychological operations."

~PSYOP

We live in an age of constant war. Our governments are at war, our ideologies are at war, our thoughts, politics and even our own ego is at war with itself. War, an organized and often prolonged conflict that is carried on between two opposing forces, in any aspect, is not glamorous. Yet, in attempting using words to describe it,

I'm doing nothing more than putting lipstick on a pig. Since my birth, the United States has engaged in war maneuvers against over 30 countries.

But, this is not a book about the history of war in the U.S. I only give you this little tidbit to plant the seed firmly in your mind the culture of aggression that is perpetuated in the country in which most of us live. Nations customarily measure the costs of war in dollars, lost production or the number of soldiers killed or wounded. Rarely do military establishments attempt to measure the costs of war in terms of individual human suffering. Psychiatric breakdown remains one of the most costly items of war when expressed in human terms. Yet, in all of this, it barely scratches the surface....

But when we talk surface-scratching.... We might be getting somewhere. Psychological effects, trauma, and operations. Also known as PsyOps. PsyOps is used across the entire spectrum of conflict, with or without any accompanying military action. It is the vampiric beast of war. Sneaking, snaking and drawing first blood. It is the wounds held below the flesh. My modus operandi.

Dutch psychoanalyst Joost Meerloo held that, "War is often...a mass discharge of accumulated internal rage (where)...the inner fears of mankind are discharged in mass destruction." Thus war can sometimes be a means by which man's own frustration at his inability to master his own self is expressed and temporarily relieved via his unleashing of destructive behavior upon *others*. In this destructive scenario, these *others* are made to serve as the scapegoat of man's own unspoken and subconscious frustrations and fears. Add in a little splash of psychological warfare and....

BINGO.

All of this information is very easy for me to share with you. It is all very heady, very educational, very dissociative and not very personal. Until the moment it is personal, then it is emotional, then... the breakdowns happen.

Enter from stage left, our next character from this story. A small insidious beast wrapped in a pink petticoat which I have affectionally named and will refer to as Polly. Polly is that chaotic, hyper-reactive, loose-cannon of a child who lives inside your mind and has teeth as tigers. She haunts you and shapes your central narratives while you are sleeping. She is the monkey mind and caused overwhelming personal and collective change from the moment she moved into my skull house. Polly thrives and grows the longer she is allowed to live in the shadows, she feeds on the emotions and shattered dreams. She is the internal masochist, whipping and lashing us from the inside. Perpetually in motion, feeding images and thoughts of re-living and happenING.

Orbiting.

Polly..... Polly.The.Sneaky.Death. PTSD. Polly who helps me disassociate everything from everything else. Polly who is responsible for me writing *you* and *them* instead of *me* and *I*. Polly, who doesn't put names on people, but labels. Makes connections just to break them. Polly, who lives in insomniatic states, chronically anxious and skittery and yet finds relaxation and calm at the bottom. Polly lives in a dream, an outside observer to the actions, and everything is on autopilot. Orbiting.

As she grew over the years, Polly's name changed. She traded in her pink petticoat when her words began to drip ferocity and blood of tooth as it sank deeply into my brain. The black terror set up shop in my soul and coursed and pumped through my marrow. Polly put on a long red dress and wrapped herself with a black leather cape lined in violet velvet. She seduced me with her beauty. This succubus, this demon who lived and breathed her words into my brain, words you will read, words that will poke you right in your virgin eyes. She is the one who opened a world of darkness and terror with ripping strands into Republican middle-America.

Polly grew into a woman within me, and wrapped her cape around my life. This black leather cape was magic. It shielded everything. It was the hard candy shell that kept me safe. Safe from everything, including my own intimate emotions. Safe from feelings, safe from everything as I bunkered into the soft velvet folds. Bunkered into my Mistress' bosom, my feelings and emotions so deeply entrenched and dug in, anger just wallowed in the pits stinking of man sweat. Psychological sieges and flashbacks were considered full-scale war, but the Mistress, with her red breast and black cape was always there, escorting me safely away. Escorting me into my dream world, into my safe-soul-space, into my zombie-state.

When a psychological siege did penetrate, the re-living happened. When the re-living happened, the walls were built higher, the trenches dug deeper, the bayonet's sharpened. Emotions became completely separate or just became non-existent. Passion and energy were re-routed into goal-directed action and arousal was no longer a cue to pay attention to incoming information.

Existence happened between the waves of frozen or over-reaction. No gap existed between stimuli and fight/flight. So avoidance was the answer. Fear, terror, helplessness and sensitivity to sound happened daily. Inhibitory feedback loops were activated to dampen a chronic state of hyper-arousal, and the thick black cape was drawn closer and tighter around my flesh.

Let me tell you something right now: Time does not heal all wounds. Time and wounds create scar tissue. Scar tissue insulates, it is organized in cellular structure and perfect. Perfectly different from its surroundings.

A perfect disaster.

A perfect performance of skin.

Learning quickly the social cues for what was expected in situations surrounded by other people. Performing. Painting the face, putting on the mask, wrapping the cape and insulated against the environmental stimuli of ordinary tasks which could trigger panic. Permanently altering my own external reality through ignoring the internal psychological war. Splitting, denial, dissociation, fantasy, vengeance and reality all living together in the trenches of war.

Death and war go hand in hand. But unlike death, War is a game of survival, survival is instinctive. An automatic response of the body.

But, the mind is always stronger than the body.

ACT II - The Deep

"Only when you slice your soul open and let it bleed
and bleed
and bleed
will you finally see your passion."

~Rae Jones

Jim, Jack, John and Jose...
...all my favorite men.

"Vi Veri Veniversum Vivus Vici"

Like any small town shattered girl, I was on auto-pilot after high school graduation. I did the obligatory. College, marriage, car and house. It's obligatory, expected. When you come from a small town, it is what you do. You get married, then have children, and go to church on Sunday. Your parents beam at their new endowment of titles Papa and Nana. They smother and love and rain attention onto the new little grand-baby of theirs. Showing and prancing and boasting to anyone who would listen.

My folks aren't that lucky. They got me instead.

I tried married.... And got divorce. But this small-town shattered girl was broken from the beginning, a broken bottle, broken mind, razor-sharp glass shard scratching at sanity. So, I did what shatters do when they hit the floor... they bounce and run. Running away from everything.

Running away from the secrets, from death, running away from the lies and trying to run away from ... well... myself. Ending up in Portland, Oregon. And as Jack White and Loretta Lynn sing it, it is exactly right.

"Portland Oregon and slow gin fizz, if that ain't love than tell me what is..."

I showed up in Portland in the fall of 2001.

It was the fall.

It was October.

I remember clearly because Portland is a dreary and grey place, sprinkled only with a few occasionally nice days between the spitting rains. I secured an apartment on the 22nd floor of a building downtown overlooking the river, watching the leaves change color. From the cold emptiness of that room I would watch the grey come in and go out day after day over the Willamette waters. It was mind-numbing and time-numbing. I found relief in the silent, still grayness of the sky. The color of the leaves changing was the only color allowed in. Sprinkling the grey with memories of Grandfather Oak, with veiny green leaves and bright sunshine.

In the grey.

You know that feeling when you are sick, the coughing scratchy throat, kind of feeling sick. The scratchy tickle-y throat that no matter how much cough syrup you drink, the tickle just won't go away? The itchiness continues until you almost want to put a wire coat hanger past your tonsils to scratch it. An itch that is just out of reach. An itch you just can't scratch. An itch that, no amount of boozy syrup would calm.

I had that itch. The bloody, scratchy, can't calm, quell or drown itch. And I scratched it, and the chrysalis of a cocoon I had wrapped myself in started to fall away. With every scratch, a piece of scabby-healed skin flaked from my mind, leaving a fresh pink claw mark in its place. In a fresh, pink, raw, city.

It was during the scratching I released the deep, seeping red, wound of love. Now, love wasn't one of those things that I went out looking for. No, my experience was that of walking through park on a sunny day and feeling something squish under my feet. Love is a bit like stepping in dog shit. Warm, squishy and yet, as soon as I noticed it and tried to rub it, clean it or otherwise get it off of me, it alternatively just spread. And... it smelled of booze and men.

I fell in love with the taste of alcohol, the smell of a man, and most of all, I liked the numbness and powerful feelings that both brought to me. The first nip of the yes-yes-yes-oh-gawd-yes, lightning in my body, let's feel this way all the time, feelings. I was a weapon. Initiated by the violence of vampiric sexuality, I was a weapon of beauty and grace and sex and seduction and secrets fueled by alcohol and fire. Lying, hiding, wound-to-tight, cat-on-a-hot-tin-roof, paranoid and jumpy. I watched and listened. Moving further and further away from normal nine-to-fiver's, I stalked in the darkest corners of life, caring less and less. I initiated the predator, the anonymous vampire, the blood-lusting, sex-fueled, psy-ops trained, deadly, silent, lioness. Oh, how I loved to keep secrets. I listened to the city, and the city told me its secrets. The secrets seduced me, and fueled my power. There were great benefits keeping those secrets. Besides my own, I kept the secrets of the powerful, rich and twisted. The blackmail. I was the Black Mistress of this city.

If you ever want to talk to a city, listen to what it has to say, then walk the streets. Day or night. Feel the concrete under your feet and it will begin to whisper. It will breathe on the breeze between the buildings, sighing in and out of alleys. A city is a living organism, and until you touch her flesh, you don't really know her. I made love to this city. I caressed her and she lived inside of me and made introductions.

The cast of characters read like that of a bad porn, and lasted about as long as a trip to the bathroom. They were my human scratching posts I left bloody and begging.

There were the vacations with the man on the yacht. Many, many vacations. Bikini's and booze and boats. He had a penchant for the perverted and was a bit unscrupulous in his requests, but ... Who am I to judge?

There was a Tour de France competitor who was married, but while the wife-y was in Scotland, he was in town *training*. Portland is, if you didn't know it, bike city. He was sweet and brought me flowers. Often. I'm not sure if he was trying to bribe my silence, or if he just really liked showering me with flowers, but... my house was filled none-the-less. Then I realized who this guy was, and why he brought me flowers and that his wife was in Scotland buying a castle.... yes, a castle. Then, he left for the Tour and I never heard from him again.

There was the Russian Mobster with the man-purse. I liked him. He taught me about the night, he taught me about the **rules** of the Night-Walkers, and showed me the underground tunnels and how to move about the city without ever setting foot on the sidewalk. He lived a high life (or low-life depending on who you asked), and nothing was out of his reach. He wasn't interested in me, but he liked having me around. He liked that I could get him things. He liked that I didn't judge him, and appreciated the acquisitions I brought him. Things like girls and drugs and money and connections. He liked that I could walk up to anyone and seduce them to our table. He liked how I could open any door that seemed to be closed. He liked that I was a day-walker and honestly, I liked hanging out with him. Bodyguards, limo's, strip clubs, and man-purses. I felt safe, respected, powerful and most of all, I felt like I could really learn how to make it in this world from him. It was difficult though, being *on call* for him and trying to hold down a day-job, but I managed. The things he was teaching were invaluable.

The connections I made were unparalleled. It wasn't until his girlfriend mysteriously disappeared one day that I thought... perhaps it was time to move on.

But, I kept in touch with the girls, the bouncers and the delivery boys.

There was the Irishman. A charming, smooth-talking, larger than life, Irish man. I met him in a conference room the day he hired me. The day-walking, power grid, seduction of an interoffice affair was too much for me to refuse.

Then, it started to rain. Rain happens a lot when you are living in the Pacific Northwest, but when it started to rain this time, it poured. I felt like anyone but Noah as the water started to rise and my life started to fall apart. The air got thick. The booze was plentiful, available and cheap. And the Irish are a good lot of heavy drinkers. A perfect recipe to get lost. Through the booze, or maybe because of it, I assisted with one of the biggest acquisition in recent company history all the while flirting dangerously with an inter-office affair. I barely got out of that company in time, with MBA in hand no less.

But, I picked up quite the habit while I was there. Lost in the booze. With each nip, my chest would radiate with a little sun inside. A radioactive center of light, my arms reaching out like bright flowers, blurring the end of my fingers. A nuclear concoction. Powerful. BOOM!

Drunk on the power, and soon, lost in the unnamed. The unnamed who loved to have a pretty girl (or two) on their arm and a drink in their hand.

Jim, the guy from the park, who i met over a bottle of Beam. Jack, the one that rode with the Gypsy Jokers and had his dick pierced - twice, who I met at a strip club over a Coke. Johnny, the other biker (the one that was married) liked his whiskey red. And Jose, The Native American that was as old as my father, shots upon shots with lime and salt. Grey Goose, Kettle One, and the hot little mulatto bar-back with the pitbull. There was the Marine, I'll have a beer. The musician, a martini please, not that one, but the OTHER musician (and that one too), with a twist. And the vagabond with a White Russian. The felons, the artists, the strippers and professionals. They were all a cocktail. They all are searching for something, all bleeding and licking their own wounds, ordering drinks, all of us looking for someone or something that would make the pain go away. Scratching at the raw pinkness of our flesh.

An escape. We were all begging to be numb.

Drinking. Drunking. Driving.

Being underwater and being drunk are very similar. Everyone seems muted, moving in slow motion, far away and glossy. Moving through air-syrup. Like how a coach on a pool deck looks through desert-stained, Vaseline-smeared goggles. Swirls of color and noise and time.

Just like I spent many mornings underwater, I spent many days and nights under booze.

When the bottles finally broke, they took my mind with them and shattered against the walls of reality. I cheered in the darkness to the faceless fuckable men (and women), the endless nights and the glass shards which littered the floor. Painful and numb. Like the shot of Novocain at your dentist's office.

They say, when you hit rock bottom, you find out exactly how strong you are. I've been there. I know rock bottom. The rocks are cool and calm under the thrashing waves. It is a calmly scary place, and I could see it coming. Looming. Flirting. So, in a moment of rational desperation, I picked up the phone.

"Hello?"
"Hey Dad."
"Hey sis."

My dad always calls me Sis. I'm not sure why and I've never asked, but I can only assume it started when my sister was born. But he has, he always has, called me sis. It has been a small endearing term of affection throughout my life.

"How's it going?"

Then, it is the small talk, the back and forth through the pleasantries trying to figure out how to say...

*Dad I'm losing it, and I'm not sure what **it** is, I need help, medication, a safe place, to be sedated, something, anything, help me.*

But, instead, saying something to the effect of:

"I'm ... not sure how I am going to make it."

I will never forget his response.

"Oh sis, don't worry, you are like a cat and you always land on your feet."

Now, I should start by saying I love my parents more than anything, but at that moment I wanted to scream. Yet, the internal mind-scream was interrupted.

"Don't worry sis, everything will work out fine."

Subdued, sedated, and more pleasantries, talks of weather, flowers, friends and then good-byes. And then...

It was the dissent. I wanted to drown and the shower wasn't deep enough. Into madness, heartbreak, depression, bottles and defiance. I'm not sure if it was that day, or a few days later. I'm not sure if a month had passed or a year, because that is what the dissent does to you, it makes space and time irrelevant. Colors blur, days become nights become days again, the rooms in your house move around and the bathroom floor is nice and cool. It is those moments that defiance creeps in.

A world war between mind and body.

My dissent was my search for an escape. An escape from the crazy, angry, bottle-filled expectations of normal. An escape into something different, something beautiful. One night, I would be safe, alone and comforted in the darkness by a voice.

"Voilà! In view, a humble vaudevillian veteran, cast vicariously as both victim and villain by the vicissitudes of fate. This visage, no mere veneer of vanity, is a vestige of the vox populi, now vacant, vanished. However, this valorous visitation of a bygone vexation stands vivified, and has vowed to vanquish these venal and virulent vermin van-guarding vice and vouchsafing the violently vicious and voracious violation of volition. The only verdict is vengeance; a vendetta held as a votive, not in vain, for the value and veracity of such shall one day vindicate the vigilant and the virtuous. Verily, this vichyssoise of verbiage veers most verbose, so let me simply add that it's my very good honor to meet you and you may call me V."

Empty bottles comforted me in my blackness fueled delirium. Comforted with movies, blankets and booze. *V for Vendetta* was playing on my TV, Natalie Portman was shaving her head to the background music of my dissent. V was my new favorite letter and my Victory. V added gasoline to an already poisoned and blackened fire. V was my savior and my destroyer. Sesame Street's letter of the day was V.

Vicodon, a pint of Vodka, a handful of Valium, a bottle of Vino, a healthy dose of defiance sprinkled with my own personal Vendetta. I was no longer afraid of death and in that was born a death-match defiance to the very core of my marrow. My anger melted in my belly of acid and alcohol. On my bed, anger melted into little saltwater pools on my pillow not deep enough to drown in. I was weightless and airborne, like a spider, resting high on the ceiling just watching the world spin below.

My last thought before everything went black:

I'd like to feel this light all the time.

The words from the TV became grainy, muted, and nothing more than a coach's voice from beneath the cap and wet. Flashes of blue from the television fade in and out of my vision, like watching the swimmers strokes above me while I lay on the bottom of the pool. Nothing is understandable, and space invades. Darkness and shadows and stars. I am floating through space. I am safe, I am alone, and I am floating through the infinite blackness of space.

When I woke up three days later. I can unequivocally tell you, I never saw God.

Just a mess. Brought to you by the letter V. Only this time, V stood for vomit.

Man-Meat

*"Divorce is a declaration of independence
with only two signers."*

~Gerald F. Leiberman

There was a man. A man of meat and bones. A man who got caught up in the grinder that was my life. The ex-husband I left behind on my one-woman show to nowhere. An average home-town boy from an average small town. Into trucks and guns and dogs and hunting and drinking beer. He spoke with snark and snuff held firmly in his lip, dry as the desert in July.

The truth was, he deserved better. We both did.

I was a broken shell, not yet grieved over the loss of my grandmother, not yet grieved over the loss of my innocence, a zombie encased in flesh and looking for a safe cave to crawl into. He was familiar, a friend since high school. He was safe. He was the sandy hole in which this ostrich buried her head in for a year. It was the calm of the sand while the waves crashed above. It was the calm mistake of thinking, *I can do this, I can keep this together*.

But, we were both so young. We got a house, and a car, and a dog. We bought things and made promises and took vacations, and thought that was the answer. Yet, we (maybe just I?) were both deeply unhappy. Expectations weighed a lot, and neither of us were built to be Atlas.

One night we went out to dinner together. Sat across a table over mexican food and margaritas.

"Do you think it is time to bring up the D-word?" I asked.

"*Yeah.*" Was his response.

"Great. I'll get the papers drawn up. Now that is over, we can go back to being friends and have a great dinner."

And we did. We laughed and talked more that night than the entire year we were married. Within a couple of weeks my things were packed and I was headed to Portland.

It wasn't that we didn't try hard enough, it wasn't that we didn't pray enough (God is a big participant in marriages where we lived). It wasn't that we didn't love each other, it wasn't any of those things. When someone asks, I have a bag full of easily-digestible half-truths. The truth is, there was no simple answer. It was complex, multi-layered and a thousand shades of grey between the black and white. I could feed you the lies of youth, of grief, of wandering eyes, of selfishness, or meddling mother-in-laws. I could tell you a thousand other excuses in which I feel expected to provide. All of these excuses hold a bit of truth, all are answers that people asking are willing to accept without much question. All of them, any of them, perhaps could have been enough to eventually drive us apart, but they are not the real answers. They are merely the symptoms.

The real question of why I got divorced should be:

"Why did you get married?"

Daywalkers

"Where do consequences lead?
Depends on the escort."

~Stanislaw Lem

The nights of hunting were long and dark, filled with people who supplied the day-walkers. The Russian was a mentor, he was like the Godfather who taught me the rules of the **other** world. The world that your mother says is *dangerous*, the world in the dark alleys which hide between the office buildings. The world of guns and mobsters and bodyguards. The world of expensive crocodile skin wallets which bulged as if they had just devoured some helpless prey. It is the world behind the curtain, and it was mine. Even after I left my association with The Russian, I still walked this world. I got nods from doormen at clubs, I called *the girls* at all hours of the night and got them *jobs* with the visiting corporate day-walkers.

Those girls were bared teeth over skeleton frames. I was the safe word, the breath of air in a life underwater. I was their opportunity for *Pretty Woman*, a champagne lifestyle in a previous existence of PBR. I was the lottery ticket to a better life, and some of them won it all.

I moved between two opposing forces like the moments between the waves on the shore. My woes were granular, moving and sloshing in the frothy waves. During the day, working the office lies, and at night, crawling the gutters with the rats. The moments between the waves my gasps and screams were heard silently by those who listened.

Heard by the city beast.

Years and years of day-walking, cubicle ants and screen savor goldfish. Excel spreadsheets, conference calls and client meetings, insurance, investments and mergers, T-times, happy hours and acquisitions. I was good at acquiring. There are truths in the day-walking world of business. In my world, it was, unequivocally, that the men are in charge. I would challenge that as many decisions, mergers, acquisitions and agreements that are made in the board room, there are an equal number which are made on the golf course, over happy hour and in health clubs. While board rooms are filled with neck-tie wearing golf enthusiasts, the rest of the office is littered with pencil skirts. A varied array of assistant skirt sizes. Skirts that go to a different bar for happy hour than the suits. Skirts filled with promises of an office, raise or partnership. A variety of skirts, wrinkled, damaged and threadbare.

Skirts attached to cankles squished into heels like only Cinderella's step-sisters could.

I wore pants.

I went to happy hour.

I learned very quickly, the neck-ties would keep me around if I could get them things. Secret, special things.

I was their own personal concierge of *special* acquisitions.

And for the skirts, I was their ear. Their liaison to the neck-ties. I was the one who would listen to them and perhaps, at times, *put in a good word* for them. I floated in this water between the skirts and the ties seamlessly. Listening, acquiring, dominating and mediating.

When the skirts would go to happy hour, I was always invited along. Then, over a few drinks salted with a splash of self-pity, I would hear stories from the skirts about being *assaulted* or *raped*. When in all manners of the truth, many of those stories are more along the lines of:

"I changed my mind the next morning when I woke up next to him"

"I was too drunk, and it felt good at the time,"

"I really wanted that raise."

To sit and listen to them... "'I've been raped twice...'"

...as they take their next drink.

I would smile, nod and listen. Secretly wanting to punch them in their little self-pity -peppered word-hole. I judged those skirts. I judged them with every ounce of spite, anger and disgust I had hidden in my shattered soul. These women were not victims of an external circumstance, they were victims first, choosing an external circumstance to reinforce their own pitiful existence. These women couldn't face taking responsibility for their own bad decisions and instead pushed blame around like unwanted creamed spinach on a dinner plate. These skirts did not get *good words* from me. These women, at an age of consent, putting themselves into a situation and then... then... changing her mind.

Crying wolf.

These day-walking women, I shake my head at and I think of my mother when she would say,

"Quit your crying, or I will GIVE you something to cry about."

Or especially,

"I brought you into this world, and I can just as easily take you out."

And the night-walking predator would scrape and claw and growl begging to be unsnapped from its tight leash inside of me. The Mistress of Death teasing me from the dark corners. Times and secret intense desires to show them just exactly what it was like. I wanted to punch and choke and kick and beat them into a bloody pulp. I wanted to reach inside their mouth with my fingers and pull out their tongues. But, I controlled.

I oozed control.

Everything was controlled.

All the while, I was reeling on the inside.

And in this controlled day-walking environment, there are some truths. In this modern time of *everyone is special*, and the ever encompassing and sweeping definition of *rape*, it is as if the line between sex and rape is blurry.

But, here is the truth. It is not blurry.

During the day, dominance, submission, aggression and passion are not rape. Miscommunication is not rape. Our first-world, holier-than-though, we-have-it-so-rough, catch-all expression, a word used to define everything that is unpleasant and disturbing about relations between any two unfair sources IS NOT RAPE. There are no universal victims with an automatic pass on everything unpleasant in life just in the name of rape.

Let me be crystal clear, SEX is not rape.

Countless of times, hearing some of these stories, I wanted to ask,

"What do you think the women in Bosnia, Croatia, the Congo, or the Sudan would say to you when you cry rape in a *Coyote-Ugly* moment?"

I wanted to scream back to them,

"What do you think the night-walking, sadistic-john-collecting women of the city would say to you right now?"

I wanted to **scream** into her perfect little sunshine world....

"RAPE IS WAR YOU STUPID BITCH!"

Rape and victimization are not the same thing.

Rape is War.

Rape is an invasive power and the imposing of psychological trauma on to someone which will effect them for years. When we start putting a context on rape and war we start to understand the detriment: War against (mostly) women, war against power, control and inadequacy. But, by exerting our power, by engaging and waging our own woman-war, with our own rules, we win. We overpower. And the cave wo-men inside the brain celebrates our own personal D-Day.

Yet, in those moments of happy hour liaison-ing, I held my tongue. Oozing control. I held my tongue with stoic control while my mind raced and cracked and judged. My mind screamed,

You cry Rape? I'll give you something to Rape about. I'll Rapey you all the way back to your little Rapey daylight-victim and booze drenched Rapey little life.

My mind raced in a way which really wanted to show them what it was like. and yet.... Silence. A smile, and another sip on a happy hour martini. Blood in my mouth from biting my tongue. Oozing bloody control. Bloody cosmos.

Over and over again.

I was angry. Angry at everyone and everything. Angry at the world, angry at my mind, angry for even opening my bloodshot and hungover eyes in the morning. Angry for having to deal with the skirts and procure for the neck-ties. Angry with the lies and half-truths, and angry for having to chew on my tongue over happy hour lemon-drops.

Until one day, one day when the blood in my mouth wasn't my own, it was a little too late, the night-crawlers were starting to invade from the shadows and her cry of wolf wasn't just a far-off cry from her voice, but a growl from my throat. Then it was just teeth and claws and fur.

I lashed.

She never cried again. None of the skirts ever cried to me again.

And the mind-shards slit at my carnal desires from the inside. Blood-drunk, filled with lust and thirsty for more.

And controlled.

And secretly.

With pants.

I hunted in the night.

The night holds everything. The night is strong and fierce and black and it was mine. I embraced it fully. The darkness was my light. It felt wonderful to drown in its embrace. I was the Queen of the Night, and the city was my slave. Like a blood-lusting vampire stealing life-force from its victims, I stole dreams, ideas, passion and desire. Swimming around in the darkness of solitary creatures of night, I felt at home. Swimming is swimming, no matter which medium.

There it is again, the faint taste of copper in my mouth. Some rooms, some times, some nights I would taste it, and it tastes like sucking on a penny. It tastes like blood. A cold piece of wet trickling down my spine. Someone died here.... or will die here, I can feel it.

You have a group of corporate investors coming into town and they are not satisfied with golf and happy hour? No problem, I will have a limo pick them up which will be fully stocked with beautiful girls, booze, drugs and an unlimited supply of options. I could move an entire party through four blocks of mazing underground tunnels without ever setting foot on the sidewalk. I had bodyguards and bootleggers, streetwalkers and smack, drivers and dominatrix's all at my fingertips.

I was a walking concierge of fantasies. Unlimited resources, unlimited supply. In my world, in my night, that is how you win a War. My war was won in a way I had tragically learned I could only win. Dominance. Power. Victimization. The prey became the predator and power was the price.

... And wars are only won when blood is spilt.

Sleeping Beauty was my favorite Disney film when I was a kid, not because I wanted to be Aurora, but because I wanted to be Maleficent. I wanted to be able to summon all the powers of hell to do my bidding all while everyone else was sleeping. I wanted to be able to transform into a fire-breathing dragon and show Prince Charming that his happy ending was just for fairy tales and stories that haven't actually ended.

Everyone wants to believe in the fairy tale. Everyone wants to hope and wish and pray and think the best. But when you live in the dark of night, you get to see the shadows everyone is hiding. The shadows are truth. If you perform by day, at night, the truth is set free. Those secrets you hope no one sees, the secrets that you keep safe with you. The secret affair you had, the secret drinks you take, the secret judgments you keep. When you have a lot of secrets, you tell a lot of lies. You hide those secrets, those dark things in your shadows, and at night, when everyone is sleeping, when they are dreaming about Prince Charming, I know those shadows take form and roam the street. And, my friend, your shadows keep me company.

Your lies kept me safe.

I loved the night-walking, street-slaying girls I hired. I loved them deeply. I held them, kissed them and protected them. Those girls knew secrets too. They were realists. I would call them if there was a particularly special *John* in town. You know, the corporate kind. The kind who would never ask his skirt to get him what I got him. The kind who pays with stacks of hundreds and orders Johnny Walker Blue and Cristal by the bottle and always likes a pretty girl on his arm. *John* would get his money's worth, and the girls, the girls would keep their mouths shut. Because... because the money was too good. My girls always had the freedom to say no, I never pressured, I just asked and gave them an option.

There were rules, there were always rules.

Always stand on his left arm, so he can shake with his right hand. Always listen, smile and appear interested and educated, but never offer your opinion unless asked. Always be nicely dressed and well-maintained but not high-maintenance. If someone asks if you would like a drink, always order champagne and drink slowly. Never smoke, curse, pick or fidget. Always stand up tall and straight and use your very best manners. Never leave his side unless he excuses himself to use the loo, only then you should also relieve yourself to powder your nose. Always remember the characters, names and conversations. At the end of your night, report back to me and you will be paid.

There were always rules.

I found my girls all over the city, in clubs, on the street, in the bookstores and libraries. Grocery stores and girl scout tables. I knew what to look for, I knew the walk. I knew to look for the beautiful disasters. The perfect hot mess. The broken reflection.

I hunted.

Hunted.

I could smell them a mile away. These girls. Trapped in bodies they loved to hate.

Some would ask, "Why?"
Some would say, "Those girls are someone's daughter."

I would reply, "Yes. And so am I."

There were some who did say no. But, those girls knew, if they said no to me, I probably wouldn't call them again. They knew that if they said yes, they would go home at the end of it with 20-large (or more) and I took 10% for my troubles. The girls could pay off student loans, child support or back rent. One night for one stack of cash.

Shame cash.

It was war, and I was a five-star general who wore the pants.

I was the yes. I was the breath between breakdowns.

Dear John, you want beluga caviar at 3 a.m. delivered to a room at the Benson? Sure. You want it delivered by a girl dressed as a nun, willing to strip you, tie you, flog you and feed it to you off of her leather encrusted feet? Sure.

I delivered.

I had people everywhere. I could get anything.
I performed.

I won.

Everyone performs for each other. We continue to do it until we are too mentally exhausted, unable or unstable to perform the act.

I controlled every minutia of detail. If the devil lived in the details, he answered to me. I took back the control that was stolen from those girls in those hours they lay in the arms of those men. I reduced those men to puppies when they begged for something specific. I made them beg. This level of control is exhausting. At exhaustion, we crack.

At exhaustion, the act is over. The final performance is done. The lights come up and the curtain is pulled away. A stage stripped bare in front of the mingling crowd, and an actor is left alone and naked without a mask.

When the cracks begin to show, that is the cue. That is the cue to get out. Because your own shadows live in those cracks. The shadows with razor sharp claws and nails and strength to reach out and grab you and pull you down. This is no fairy tale, and these are not happy endings. You get out, or you go down. I saw both.

And one day ... my crack started seeping.

I got out, and focused on something else. Anything else. Always looking over my shoulder. It was the days, and the day-walkers. Distract myself with the light. Distract myself with the mind-numbing, Novocain induced days. Day after day after day, numb.

Comforting myself with the lies. When the days are long, those lies are longer. So the Irishman and I packed a bag and headed to the ocean. It was my birthday, and nothing is better than the Oregon Coast in January on your birthday.

Waves

Like as the waves make towards the pebbl'd shore,
so do our minutes, hasten to their end.

~William Shakespeare

The Oregon Coast in January is tragically beautiful. It is storms and sea, waves crashing and clouds lashing and the perfect place to celebrate the birthday of a fucked up girl trying to find the bottom.

I know it was my birthday, but I couldn't tell you what number I was celebrating. Those years seem to blur together and time gets a little bit fuzzy in the memory banks.

I remember we stayed at this old place called the Ester Lee Motel. It was a hotel that was not much more than a forgotten mom-&-pop shop wrapped in wood paneling with an ocean view. Each room had a fireplace and functioned to be cozy and warm like grandma's handmade quilt and a cup of tea when you are sick. The Ester Lee looks like it walked out of 1975 with charm and grace and could have been featured as the perfect vacation spot for the *Brady Bunch.* It was everything good you remembered about childhood wrapped in walls. It was road-trips and board games, hugs and cookies. The Ester Lee was the embodied perfection of what could have been.

It was just a short walk down the beach from the Inn at Spanish Head.

The Inn at Spanish Head however, was everything contemporarily opposite to the comfort of Grandma Ester Lee's living room. It is a sprawling resort, glamourous and untouchable. It has meeting facilities and spa services, room service and wedding packages. It is wired with wifi, cable TV and has it's own *App* for your *Iphone* to easily navigate. It is anonymous, cold, grand, beautiful and impersonal.

With just a short walk between these two places, my entire life had functioned much like the waves on the same shore. Pushed and pulled, here then there. Wanting both at equal and opposite times. Jutting rocks slashing themselves out of the ocean. Foam and froth and spray trying to grab them and pull them back in. Storms of a bruised sky looking to seek revenge on its salty attacker. The comfort of sand and sun on the shore. Warm and welcoming, cold and calculating. Day versus Night. Light versus Dark. Angels and Demons and Fairies and Vampires.

I remember we left the comfort of our Ester Lee blanket and went to the Inn for my Birthday dinner, walking along the beach at sunset to the restaurant. It was astonishingly clear the whole weekend, an anomaly in January. The waves were loud, ominous and crashing, but there wasn't a cloud in the sky. We had spent the afternoon drinking beer in the sand and watched the sunset over spritzers. We got to the restaurant and nibbled appetizers over aperitifs, drank dinner through wine bottles, and dove into dessert with the lascivious gluttony of bottles upon bottles of brandy. Everything was the washed out color of the moon streaming through the windows. Pale and silvery: walls, ceiling, chairs, the people moving, sitting, eating and talking to each other like ghosts. Ghosts of the flesh, invisible people moving around like oversized ants.

We drank that slippery sand bar dry till closing.

I took sips of whatever was placed in front of me and instantly loved the burn. The soft pear flesh cooking in sugar boiling on my insides. I loved how the drinks were nearly undrinkable. A potion that changed me, made me brave and strong, the glow warming my belly and spreading throughout my body like the moon on the ocean reflecting through the other side of the glass.

I was underwater before we even got to the ocean. Underwater all afternoon, underwater over dinner and dessert. Underwater again when that sneaky wave interrupted the romance of a perfectly good, black-nighted, drunken, sandy-stumble back to the hotel.

I can hold my breath a long time.

It was tragically beautiful. Drunk and tumbling in the birthday-wish frosting of black sea froth under the stardust of night. Night-walking is like that tumble. It is that swim on the Oregon Coast at midnight in the middle of January. It is numbingly cold pitch-blackness that is comforting on a drunken walk. It is jarring like a sneaker wave.

I swam out into the ocean. Swam until the stars were shining brighter than the lights on the shore. Diving deep under the waves, I swam to silence the voices. To drown death herself. I dove down and opened my eyes. Digging my hands into the grains of sand at the bottom.

I have a string of my Grandmother's pearls. A string of smooth oyster sea-sand on rope. Irritations turned into perfection over time, strung together as jewelry. She touched it, wore it, and it still smells like her. Sometimes when I feel lonely, I will caress the string carefully, smell it delicately and use it like my own personal rosary. Praying to hear her voice again. Praying I could call her, hug her and play cards. The ocean jewels are my way of touching her. There is no piece of stone with her name on it that I can trace with my fingertips. She is just ashes. The color of sand. She lays beneath a tree in front of her home. Grass grown over and family having long since moved away. Another family lives there now, with my grandmother's ashes feeding a living pink Dogwood in their yard.

I want to go there and dig up the dirt. I want to hold her in my hands again. I have no pictures, just pearls. Pearls in the oceans. The sand is ash slipping through my fingers. The waves of the ocean between the Esther Lee and the Inn at the Spanish Head was my life. Sandwiched between the crisp cold darkness of sky and sand, warmth and coolness, the sea within me.

My bobbing little head surfacing in rhythm with the waves for a breath, then under the water I would go, sloshing around on the bottom with the fish. I would close my eyes real tight in the dark wetness and push all of the air out of my body until I felt as though I was a stone in the sand. I did this often in the summer, laying on the bottom of an Olympic-sized pool like a black piece of tile, watching the way the sun turned into three shining crystalline stars through the chlorine kaleidoscope. Watching the swimmers above me go back and forth, casting moving shadows on my body. Holding my breath for as long as possible.

You can tell a lot about a person by watching them swim. You can tell if they were ever a competitive swimmer. If they ever spent endless summers in a pool staring at tiles. You can tell because of a certain repetitiveness and gracefulness to the stroke as their arms lift out of the water. As if when the person hits the wet, their hands turn to paddles and legs like fins. Then, by watching closer, by watching their breath cadence you can tell if they swam indoors or outdoors. You can tell if they found peace in the heavy air of humidity and chlorine of an enclosed pool, or found freedom in the silence and cold/warmth of the water while elements thrashed against the rubber swim-cap and goggles of the unpredictable outside-edness.

That cold night, the Irishman was 6'3" and 250lbs of muscle beating the living crap out of those waves. He was NOT a swimmer. I watched him. He was a fighter. He never dove under, he never took his eyes off me as he struggled closer. His arms chopping at the waves like an ax on a huge wooden block. I just kept swimming. To a new life, a new body and a new nightmare. Something. Anything, and honestly, nothing at all. I just wanted to be underwater and swim no where. No fish. No Mermaid. No God. No breath.

Before we are born, we are all swimmers. Before we breathe, we swim. Before we have bones and thoughts and brains and shoes, we swim. We are all the same, coming from the same space dust, the same spermy little swimmer, the same breathable amniotic life. All before earth and air and bodies trap us.

And... in the water, I felt free again. Whoever I walked as on land, that person disappeared when I gained the freedom of the infinite blueness of the water. I gained the life, and the breath and the blue. It flowed through me. It was oneness and acceptance and everything the air and earth wasn't.

He, however, did not look free that night.

So I swam. Out in those cold ocean waves with my jeans and my cable knit sweater pulling me backwards, dragging me down. I swam towards newness, towards coldness, towards the fish and the blackness of sky and sea separated only by the white froth of the waves.

I swam until the club of a hand attached to the Irish-water-thrasher grabbed the coarse cable-knit of my sweater. As drunk as I was that night, I'll never forget that moment. It was like Thor himself sent a shock of electric reality striking me right on the neck. I went limp. I didn't fight or struggle and I didn't help by swimming back. I just lay limp at the end of his cable-knit encrusted fist like a rag doll. Getting thrashed around by the waves, I watched the stars dance in the sky through the froth on my face as my time of wet passed by. I was dragged, not so gently, back to the shore. By the time we hit sand, he was exhausted thanks to my non-help, and I just howled at the moon. Laughing, I rolled around in the sand before staggering to my feet and leaving a trail of soaking wet clothes down the beach towards our hotel. Until I was naked and alone, wolf-wailing like a crazed wild animal at the moon and stars.

I realized that night, there are many ways to drown, many ways to run away and many, many ways to breathe.

The Light

"I have harnessed the shadows that stride from world to world to sow death and madness."

~H.P. Lovecraft

Post-bender and broken in many ways. I had $70 to my name and was drowning in debt. Debt left over from a divorce, debt from being unemployed and dysfunctional. But none-the-less, this debt had followed me (and on occasion, bit me) like a little lost dog right down to the bottom.

Then the *yes* moment happened. The breath moment. The moment where something comes along and you aren't sure if it looks good or not, but it is definitely better than where you are, and you say yes. The *yes* moment is the breath between the waves, the moment where you see clear blue sky and fill your lungs with air and every thing is perfect. Just for one moment. My *yes* moment came in the option of setting up the administration of a new business. It came in the option of getting sober. It came by doing some bookkeeping, some office management, some schedule coordination and before I knew it, also publishing a quarterly magazine full of events, articles and activities. The *Yes* moment happened, the business happened, and sobriety happened.

But, this was not just any business, but a business built on (wait for it) woo-woo. Now, I use the term woo-woo as endearingly, affectionately and yet as completely tongue-in-cheek as possible. To **woo** is to make someone fall for you, to make them like you. Woo-woo is based on or involving irrational superstition. My **Woo-Woo** was both, it was, quite honestly, 10,000sq feet of space specializing in a seductive spiritual smorgasbord.

It is a world of demons and angels, fairies and vampires, the epitome and personification of the ongoing battle of light and dark. *It* was exorcisms and empowerment. *It* was the *cheat code* the *power module* the *Law of Attraction,* and *Eckart Tolle. It* was Meditation, Initiation, and Ritual. *It* was spirituality and *Warriors of Light.* **It** was sobriety and energy, and **It** was secrets.

Lots and lots of secrets.

Now, besides my own perfected foray, I come from a long line of secret holders. 3rd (and 33rd - depending on the order)-degree Masons have lived and breathed in my family line like the DNA itself which runs through my veins. Swords, rings, ceremony and fraternal orders are passed down as family heirlooms. Names like *DeMolay* and *Robert the Good* pepper the lineage. It is a tradition, for the men. I was the first born in the line, yet, not a boy. So, I sought my secrets elsewhere. In a familial line of Knights Templar the internal desire for a peek behind the curtain wasn't tempered because I had a pussy rather than a penis. Instead, it just added passion to the pursuit.

My first college degree came in history with a focus on ancient religions. My years in college were accented with studies in sociology, Paganism, anthropology and Wicca (Initiated as a High Priestess after 2 years and 2 days). Shamanism (Sweat Lodges, a Vision Quest and finally an invitation to pull the buffalo skulls – to which I politely declined) and Ancient Persian rites of passage (Thank you Dr. Shabazi). I was well-read in the practices and beliefs of the Norse, Egyptians and Zorastrians.

So, I didn't go into this spiritual quest blind, nor empty-handed. Yet what I found was entirely different from what I was expecting.

In all my early years of deep searching, I found teachers welcoming me with open arms and patience in the inquisitive nature I peppered them. Balance and calm in the frenzy of desperate digging for meaning. Listening rapt to the voices of these teachers from all over the world, infusing words with shades of deeper meaning.

Much deeper than I could ever find in a book.

With my *It* moment, this time was different.

Different because I was building a business and remodeling a 10,000 sq ft building at the same time. Different because, from the beginning, the Initiations came quickly, the *activations* without impunity and I climbed the ranks. It was fast and quicker than what had been seen in the past, quicker than normal and quicker than what was recommended. When I jumped, I went directly into the deep end and over my head.

In the deep, there was a peace. A peace I was familiar with. A peace in the hours spent in meditation. A peace in the calm of the Temples I visited all over the world. Peace sitting on the tiles of the deep end. Peace swallowing me like a pond to a stone. Peace in ignoring the outside world. Peace in the thought that I found a place, a place to expunge my soul, a place of acceptance and healing of self. Peace in this reflective calm of the water. Peace in my own personal Temple.

All of this is true.

Until *It* isn't.

There was GREAT power in these Initiations. More than I could adequately explain or even imagine. *It* started in December of 2006 and by the end of 2007, I completed 5 Initiations, traveled to three countries, spent over $20,000 in *spiritual training* all while helping run the center. It was 80 hours a week of working, plus my own personal spiritual steeple chase. I had climbed the ranks, whether through hard work, lineage, natural ability, talent or an ability to keep secrets, I'm not sure.

It wasn't long before I was included in *International Leadership Meetings, Master Teacher* panels, and conducting these sacred Initiations of my own, with the same familial sword passed down over the generations that my paternal line has held so sacred.

The Initiation ceremonies were powerful. They were Holy, they were everything that was perfect about empowerment. These Initiations tapped into something unexplainable, something powerful, something deep, and something ancient. It was an awareness. It accessed and opened a channel that otherwise would have remained shut. I was given a magic name which unlocked and unleashed all of my hidden power within. A secret code to tap into the ancientness of magic which surrounded me. It woke something inside and immediately altered my perception.

It was my religious awakening filled with weekend spiritual warriors.

I participated in secret and holy Temple rituals and Egyptian rites of passage. I learned the Enochian Language, the language of the Angels. I was a participant in summoning powers which were so much greater than my humanness. Powers of Universal proportions.

In Enochain magic, the highest light in the Temple is at the Watchtower. The purest form of being-ness held at the lifeguard stand.

When light hits water it creates unity. It creates reflections. It creates blinding white.

Water.

A structure unlike any other in the Universe. The singular structure which manifests in three states. Gas, liquid and solid. Water is willing to accept any state, any time and in any form. Two foreign entities coming together in perfection. In unity. To create, and to reflect.

Do you want change? You need to get in the water.

Light against this water creates all spectrum. It creates the entire spectrum of color and sound. Creating is a secondary function of unification.

Speaking is a secondary function to breathing.

You cannot work magic, you cannot be a catalyst for change, you cannot move anything without deeply understanding this. Breath will carry feelings you have never felt before, experiences you have never had. The key to everything is breath. It is tantra. It is life.

I deeply understand.

It was a look behind the curtain to the great energetic machinery in which we live. I got to crank the wheel of manifestation.

A Temple.

A golden pyramid. Only the mind of Buddha opens the door, then seals the operations of the Temple. Once you take the steps in, it will be sealed in the Temple for life. Every step. Every breath, is sealed.

TaDa!

It caused profound and powerful change. It delivered what I had hoped.

Let me say again, there is great power in these Initiations. The more Initiations received, the more power is leveraged. With great power, comes great responsibility, and like many of the famous internal struggles of good vs. evil in our modern-day superheros, I found that to be true in this case as well.

A golden pyramid.

A loaded gun.

Then, *It* began showing through the skin. Showing through the Earth-suit of empowerment.

No one is perfect. Especially people and groups with so much power. I learned first hand that although these Initiations came with power, it did not change a person's nature. It did not change their desire. It did not automatically create Holiness like the Dali Lama or compassion like Mother Theresa. You should know by now, the deeper you go, the darker the water gets. In the deep, light is just a mere shadow in the blue. As calm as it might look on the surface, the strength below moves fast and churns secretly, and shadows roam the street.

I was always good at finding the shadows, they had kept me company for so long I could say hi to them as I passed on the street. Those shadows were my friends. The dark energy. The mistress, demons and exorcism. I was pretty good at exorcism too. The Mistress of Death was still at my hip. So I danced and lived within the shadows, tricked them into being my friends and was the escort of light.

A Mistress of purification. With water. Holy Water.

The Purification by Light Ritual
(as used in exorcisms)

Ateh, Ateh, Atoi Libre
Amma, Amma Atoi Libre,
In Nomani Elohim
In Nomani Spiritus Sancti
In The Name of the Light
May It Shine
May It Shine
May It Shine

Ohm Mani Padme Hum
(chant for 3-5 minutes)

The shadows are always the ones that can slip between the worlds. As you breathe, as you sink into yourself, into the shadows, blend in with the darkness. It is easy to hide, and people will forget you are even in the room. They are just so blinded by the lights. In the Temple, in the shadows, invisible, with a loaded gun.

Purified. Exorcised in Water. Breathing in the dark.

A class started, the teacher was introduced and the first words he said were:

"I will lie to you. It is your job to figure out the truth."

Whoah! Hold on. What? I didn't sign up for a lie-detector course. What part does lying play in empowerment?

A sense of ill-fated-ness crept over my skin. Little invisible, ill-fated army ants charging up from the earth and creeping north invading my secret, special and vulnerable little spots.

"You will have to get through the lies to get to the next step. Only through the lies will you learn to have faith in yourself."

And then... I knew.

I was finally starting to see behind the curtain of this Universal machinery. What I found, in the empowerment cloaked belly of this beast, wasn't any worse that what I had seen or been involved in. It was worse because of depth and knack, so they say, of verisimilitude. The hope of redemption and light, the appearance of being true. It was a perfected illusion that had been so seamlessly put in place to make it appear like it was the answer to what ailed you. On the surface, it was. But, in the darkness of the deep, the shadows roamed freely.

An Oscar-worth performance of epic proportions. Layers and layers of lies. Layers of illusions and shadows and secrets. It only takes a few bad apples to spoil the bunch.

The holiest of rituals were tainted with irreverence. Spitting on the sacred cow. Turning Sacred Sexuality and ancient holy Tantric teachings into prostitution, orgies and a sanctified sex trade. The deeper I got, the darker it was. Tax evasion, blackmail, degradation, abuse and dare I say murder? All for sport, all behind the curtain, all under the ruse of empowerment.

What I thought was so good and pure, the turquoise blue of the ocean waves, was nothing but a hiding place of the deep secrets that would even make Cthulhu shiver. The dichotomy of the waves between empowerments and exploitation, healing and abuse left many gasping for air. The only peace found was in the silence of laying on the stones in the deep of meditation, breathing underwater and watching the waves crash above.

"She could be so powerful if she just could get her sexuality under control."

Under control? A comment I heard a so-called Master Teacher utter about me. Her own judgements and insecurities sharpening the barbs which left her tongue. I didn't need "fixing" or "healing", I didn't need to get "my sexuality under control," I was VERY much in control. Beyond being in control, I was an OCD control freak, and because of that (or maybe in spite of it), I gladly fueled an already active rumor mill. The stories were sordid, the rumors were wildfires, but the truth... the truth was much less entertaining.

As playful and flirtatious of a performance I might have put off in public, the open-mindedness and acceptance in other's sordid sex lives, sent tongues wagging. The truth was, I was chaste. Perhaps chaste is not the correct word. Maybe the correct word is more like.... Not.

At that time, I was not fucking anyone. Not making love, not having sex and a whole host of other *not's* I was accused of doing. I was sober. I was chaste. I was happy laying on the bottom shooting air bubbles from the deep. There was nothing happening with those who I was accused of having it with. The internal alarm was ringing, the knowing that at any moment there will be a predator and a victim. It is the *when* and *who* that produce the most tension.

Men pitting women against each other. Men solidly putting into place a glass ceiling in which NO woman could breach. Well, that isn't true. You could breach it, if you slept with the right man. If you slept your way to the top, if you did what he wanted you to do. The price of the most deeply held secrets was sex. Or money. You could work for free. Slavery or sex. Two options for the price of empowerment.

I have played this game before. This is MY war.

"Well, if you aren't going to sleep with me, then I am going to hire a hooker and have sex right in front of you. I am going to call one of the MANY girls I have in this city." He yelled at me.

We had shared a suite at L'ermitage in Beverly Hills, 700 sq ft of space separated two rooms. All locked behind one door and a short elevator ride up from deal-making central in Los Angeles. Marble bathrooms and a private balcony with a saltwater pool on the roof. Luxury at its finest.

"That's fine," I said, shrugging my shoulders and going back to the book I was reading. "Need me to dial the phone for you?"

He fumed, and I held my ground. He walked toward me, his eyes were so vacant it just seemed that his soul had just floated away. This was my teacher? When he raised his hand, I said,

"You better make it good, because it will be the last time you ever touch anyone. Ever."

...and I meant it. My teeth growing like sharp sickles with each syllable. Saliva collecting in my mouth.

Watering.

He sized me up. Just stood there and stared. I never moved. I didn't flinch, I never dropped his eyes. I set my jaw and could feel the energy of the Dark Death with me, hovering around me like some invisible protector. My black, shadow-fueled, death cape of war. A war I could win.

That night changed everything.

He huffed, turned on his heel and his body looked like that of a two-year old getting ready to throw a temper-tantrum. I just sat there watching. He walked to the wet bar and poured himself a drink. One drink turned into many and when there was no more alcohol to be had, he passed out. I could hear the great wall-shaking snores from my room all night.

For the first time in my life, I was not the Mistress, the adulteress or the floozy. I was not the madam or the victim. I was not lying. I was free of the guilt, the shame and the hiding. Yet.... ironically, the fingers kept furiously pointing. The shit-storm was dog-piling quicker than a quarterback sack.

Apparently, the lies from a mans lips weigh more than the truth from my own. And like any other time, when you are caught under the weight of a man, it is hard to breathe. His true mistresses were protected, while I was hung out to dry. Once lauded for my beauty, those same people used it to attack, and when they did, it was vicious. I personified their own shame. I embodied their own indiscretions.

A woman who was cheating on her boyfriend cast fingers at my *adulterous* nature.

An insecure wife pulled me aside in the middle of dinner to threaten me and say, "Stay away from my husband." To this day, I am still not quite sure what she was talking about.

A husband who was having an affair with his secretary had painted a target on my back (The secretary was oh-so-happy to protect herself through my lynching).

Others who knew the truth were too afraid their own secrets would show if they opened their mouths. So I burned.

"Burn the witch" so they say.

"Burn the witch because she didn't drown."

Ostracized.

Cast out.

Orbits in October.

I did nothing wrong, and found myself alone in a fight for my good name and reputation. The breaking point happened in December of 2009 when I started receiving death threats. Stress was already working it's magical destructive touch upon my body. I was down to 127lbs (at 5'10"), my hair was falling out and now I was receiving threats of a murderous nature.

All alone.

People who had promised to have my back, people who had committed to *always be there for me no matter what*, friends who made promises, brothers who strength I lacked, weren't there when I needed them most. In an organization of light-workers, the days were becoming quite dark.

I filed restraining orders and consulted with a bodyguard. I documented everything and when I finally left the organization, it was with a stack of cash to keep quiet. A large, heavy stack of shame-cash to go away silently.

I have files full of paperwork dated back to 2007. I kept notes on everything. Dates and times and conversations and every single email. Even the ones I promised I would delete. I kept them all. If there were promises of friendship and loyalty made, I had kept insurance for when those promises were broken.

And...

True to form...

They were.

I knew these humans better than they knew themselves. The darkness always holds the truth. It is under the brightest of lights where the greatest performances take place. But the brighter the lights on stage, the darker the shadows grow behind you.

I left because I was abandoned by the people I trusted the most. Abandoned to drown in the dark waters of blame, held under by the weight of others shame. Drowning.

In an organization focused on empowerment and energy, many don't realize the tremendous destruction which is left in the wake of their own insecurities.

Leaving an organization that had become so intimate in my life, that had become so empowering on so many levels, was hard. Being brandished with an "A" was harder, but the hardest thing of all was losing my friends. The friends who I had held as my closest confidants. My friends who were my family. These friends who I shared secrets and tears with, laughter and advice. These were the friends who were the first people allowed inside my hard little broken shell of a soul. The friends who looked at this mosaic of emotional catastrophe and slipped between the cracks like smoke. Yet, after all of it, there is no loyalty among thieves.

A stack of cash does not replace the things I lost.

Overnight.

With no warning.

It didn't take much more before I began to question my belief in the goodness of human nature. I questioned my belief of everything. Quickly realizing the only thing I believed in was water. Water unifies, water reflects, water creates and I believe in the truthfulness of the wet.

One of the last notes I made from this time was:

"A quietness you can't teach, a stillness in body, mind and spirit. Where the only movements, thoughts and actions are set into motion through will and a conscious connection with a higher power. An energy set forth for the absolute progression of human consciousness."

Humans are 80% water. I believe it. I believe that our lives are reflected through others. This human-water can be a deep indigo blue or shallow turquoise but either way when the sun hits it just right, there is always a reflection, always color and always a shadow.

I Don't.

"I do."

~The Married

It is a strange feeling. Standing at the back of an aisle, in a tiara and with flowers and dressed as a white princess, looking at a long walk of expectations in front of you knowing what you are supposed to feel. You are supposed to feel like a princess in a fairy tale with her happily ever after within reach. You are supposed to be excited and nervous and happy and fresh and new and clean. It is your day, your happily every after. But instead, saying...

"Dad, I can't do this."

Hearing back with a proud, deep voice, strong arm and a beaming smile,

"It's okay sweetheart, it will be fine, that's just cold feet."

Wanting to trust him, wanting to believe that yes, in fact, it was going to be okay. Yes, it was just cold feet. He believed it. He knew. He had been there. But he was so far away from me. I was instead, confused, knowing it was wrong, feeling it was wrong, but not comprehending how I got there in the first place, and not knowing the words to say it. I was lost.

The last thing I remember clearly was about eight months ago my beloved grandmother laying in cold purple pajamas, surrounded by smells of pungent flowers and embalming fluid, birds of paradise and lost hope.

Lost.

This is all happening so fast. If it wasn't my fairy tale, then whose life was I living? Wait. Where am I? Why am I dressed in this? Wait! Stop! I can't breathe.....

A wrongness surrounded me, like an alarm clock had gone off without being set. Walking. Step by step. Guided down a long-short aisle. Frozen and moving in fear. I was trapped in the waves of a wedding Tsunami getting churned in a washing machine of family, friends, flowers, a blur of white and handed off to a boy with blonde hair in a tuxedo.

"If anyone thinks these two shall not get married, speak now, or forever hold your peace."

Someone, somebody, please say something.

My eyes searching the room, scanning, begging, and standing in front of a man, in front of an altar, in a room called "Romeo and Juliet", drinking the poison, dying, in front of 30+ members of family and friends, on a cruise ship.

Living a lie.

Living the expectation.

Performing.

"I do."

"I do."

WHAT?! NO! WAIT! STOP! I CAN'T BREATHE!!!! My body has betrayed me! How did I get here?

Tormented inside. Reeling and scared, shattered and already broken before it even began. Not knowing the words, living the expectations of the tightly wound braid of conservatism, all-American-ness and Republican God-faring-people around my neck. Standing there and living through the belt of the Bible that bared down and lashed upon my flesh.

One year, One month and 10 days later, we decided to get a divorce over a strangely calm dinner of Mexican food and margaritas. My body eating stress and grief like a diabetic eats a donut. My muscles chronically tight, like a tight rope walker taking his first step without a net, resting anxiously against my bones.

Without telling anyone, I packed a suitcase and got in my car and headed out to the open road, out onto the freeway. I drove and drove and drove. I looked for this place called the *way of free*, I looked and watched and walked. There was no freedom, just a ghost of flesh watching people mingle and move. Driving hard, thinking the rubber on asphalt would miraculously fix something on the inside. Driving 200 miles away, one way, then turning around and driving 500 miles in the opposite direction. Trying to regain some balance in a life which was spinning dangerously out of control. 800 miles and counting of back and forth uncontrolled, shattered, and spinning tires.

I divorced this small town dripping with expectations with a Fed-Ex envelope, a note to have it signed and a check to have it filed at the county clerks office. But, even with Fed-Ex fueled rubber patches on brain shatters, balance was still far far away, and spinning was the new normal.

Divorced people understand deeply that a marriage isn't a guarantee of anything, and Portland, Oregon is a great town for drowning in a slow-gin fizz.

Burn, Baby, Burn

*"The atoms that make up the human body, are traceable
to the crucibles that cooked light elements into
heavy elements in their core under extreme
temperatures and pressures.
These stars- the high mass ones among them- went
unstable in their later years- they collapsed and then
exploded- scattering their enriched guts across the
galaxy- guts made of carbon, nitrogen, oxygen, and all
the fundamental ingredients of life itself...
So that when I look up at the night sky, and I know that
yes we are part of this universe, we are in this universe,
but perhaps more important than both of those facts is
that the universe is in us."*

~Neil deGrasse Tyson

When the bottom hits, it hits hard. After a Vendetta-
fueled bender of a night, waking up in a pool of vomit,
blood, piss, spit and shit, I knew I needed to make some
serious changes.

So, I did. I did when I decided to get sober. Decided to go on a full-out cleanse of body, mind and spirit.

Woo to the capital WOO.

I was completely sober for three years. It was a profound. After being pretty constantly drunk for the previous six, it was Ecstatically-Enlighten-ly profound. When I decided to do it, I didn't just decide to get sober. I decided to run screaming to the other end of the sober spectrum. Nazi-sober. I was more sober than a Mormon on Sunday.

By 2008-(ish) I was in the midst of exploring mind-bending psudo-scientific healing techniques, I was pursuing en-LIGHT-en-ment with energy force. Esoteric rituals and secret societies, crystals, wands and activations. Magic and Initiations from an ancient time. I drank the Kool-Aid. I breathed and meditated and ignored the mainstream. I moved in with aliens and angels and neo-woo-woo-new-age-hippy-dippy-spiritually-enlightened *warriors*. It was gluttonously wonderful. It was my dry in the alcohol of wet. It was my displaced addiction to escape. I had just traded one for the other and headed to the furthers point I could.

Then, as any crazy, middle-of-sobriety, not-in-touch-with-reality, ecstatic, enlightened, sober-for-three-years person would do, I committed to traveling 1000 miles to the middle of the Nevada desert to spend a week at the **BIGGEST** rave/ party/ orgy/ drug-fueled/ dust-filled/ enlightening/ esoteric experiences on the planet.

It was Burning Man.

It was 2009 and the theme was "Evolution."

It was right up my woo-woo infested alley.

There seems to be two kinds of people in this world. People who have heard of Burning Man and have gone (or want to go) and people who haven't. And don't.

I had always wanted to go. ALWAYS. From the time I could remember hearing whispers about it as early as 1995. I wanted to go to this magical place where booze and drugs and hedonism ran rampant. I wanted to participate in this feast for the senses, this Disneyland for adults. I wanted to feel and taste and touch and smell and experience everything and anything. I wanted to dive into the ocean of bliss and drown in the ultimate escape for ten days.

I wanted to lick the sky.

Ecstasy.

I was going.

And... I was sober. And... I was chaste.

It was Burning Man.

Burning Man, for those who don't know, is a cross between Woodstock, MardiGras, Carnival in Rio, New Year's Eve in Times Square, Halloween in Lahaina, Macy's Thanksgiving day parade, the World Krishna Conference, Holi in India, the Super Bowl and virtually every other totally-off-the-wall event, parade, holiday, festival or costumed event you have ever been to, seen or heard of.

Times ten.

Humorous, bizarre, absurd, beautiful, outrageous, loud profane, weird, dirty, hot, cold and dusty. *Cirque de Soleil* meets *Mad Max*. The most hedonistic conglomeration of wonderful, naked, writhing, grateful, honest, profane, humanity imaginable. Hundreds upon hundreds of sprawling camps, each one more elaborate, strange and original. Thousands of installations dotting the sun-cracked desert floor, each more colorful, intricate, creative, mind-boggling and spectacular than the next. Art, music, religion and cooperation that one must experience and absorb to even begin to fully comprehend.

Times ten.

Then times ten again.

Words can't paint a picture of Burning Man, just like a cloud can't drive a car. It is everything you could never quite conceive of and certainly cannot describe.

Burning Man is in this space, this space between the space where those pieces of life billow through you. The pause between the in-breath and out-breath. The rip in space and time. It is there where you learn to feel how other people are feeling. Where you find hope, and healing and touch and connection and oneness, like sparkling stones at the bottom of dark water. Separate, but together, in the dark water of the desert with monsters.

To get to this magical place, the terrain is rocky, the roads are marked with gravel, open range signs and cattle guards. And then... it is flat. Flat for miles and miles and miles with nothing but baby powder fine dust, stars and more dust. And then, like stardust, out of the desert, a mirage. Like a modern day Bedouin traveling in a caravan to a magical oasis.

The Holy Land.

A modern day Mecca.

50,000 people traveling from all over the world traveling in on one dusty road to create a city for one week, only to let it burn and disappear again on the wind leaving no trace. Not even a trace of one speck of glitter. Passing ghost towns along the way filled with perplexed residents wondering why anyone, let alone 50,000 of anyone's would want to camp out in the desert for a week and drown in the dust. But that is exactly what it is...

Drowning in star-dust.

Ten days. Sober. Chaste. With shirt-cocking fashion shows, nipple clamps and pole dances, aliens, costumes, enlightenment, headlamps, chapstick, sunblock, water, and shade structures built with cars, tapestries and rebar like some *Mad Max* version of circling the wagons.

Tutu's and glowsticks, lemons and leather, zip-ties and ziplock, fake flowers and fire. Lots and lots of fire. Everything is burned. Camps, men, temples, furniture and dreams.

All of it burns.

The flames lick at the star-dust and char the ground. The fire burns away the impure, and transmutes the past. The phoenix rises and so does the devil himself. It is transmutation in the physical. All covered in dust.

There is dust. baby-powder-fine dust on everything. Goggles and masks, camel-paks and tarps, trampolines and pussy pancakes. Glory Hole Hot Dogs and Barbie Death camp/Wine Bistros. If you can imagine it, it is there.

Times ten.

Sober.

Covered in stars and dust.

I saw the sun rise in the desert through goggles once more. The sun looks exactly the same when it rises, no matter what desert you watch it rise in. No matter how old you are. The sky aflame with pink, blue, purple and orange hues. The air hung a slight chill over my fur covered shoulders. But, there was no Unicorn this time. Sure, there were lots of unicorns, but not MY Unicorn.

There were no Greek Gods.

There was no orchestra of whistles and gasps and bubbles.... those days were long since past. Just pumping music, fire and an ocean of dust and stars.

Out at the edge of the Universe, standing on this dust, looking as the bright star replaced the dark stardust, it was silent. Silent like the wail of a sirens call shattering the armor in my soul.

At the apex of the week, the Saturday night - the man burns... **The Burn**. The man in flames. It is chaos. And is, by far, the wildest pyrotechnics display on the planet.

Times ten.

Times another ten.

And again. Times. Ten.

It is total chaos, fire-dancers, fire-eaters, drunken screaming, ecstasy fueled pumping, the waves churning and I can feel everything rise up inside of me with the Phoenix.

The panic I foolishly thought was gone, the darkness I had breathed and breathed and meditated and stupidly thought I had vanquished by some miraculous sobriety-fueled, energetic, light-infused, alien-landing, healing technique.

No.

Not gone.

There is still dark water. There is always dark water. When you are born in the darkness, the darkness never leaves.

Dark water a 1000 miles from no where, in the middle of no where, dressed in fur, glow lights and techno, surrounded by 50,000 people screaming. There are men on fire and lights attached to nipples and, and, and, and chaos and, and, and....

You. Are. Sober.

In chaos. Over-under stars'-dust. Surrounded by flames.

The perfect place for panic-attacks.

The internal mind-shard, crackled, crushed, shattered and the fight for breath was beginning once again.

Sober.

Drowning in the dust. I put my goggles on. They help me breathe. I can see where I am going. But it doesn't make it stop. Panic attacking like some sledge-fisted monster. Hammering away at me, hammering the air out of my lungs. All I could think was....

Get in the tent. Into the bag. Hide.

Still and silent, while the world outside raged in a tornado of techno and taint. Crawling inside of myself to shush the screams of my soul. Shush the screams of the demons which bounced to each oonze oonze oonze in the air. Shaking, shivering and scared. The ground was soft and cold, the walls of the tent blew in and out like great cheeks puffed with air. A tent trying to breathe underwater in the desert. Math games, breath counts...

1000 miles from home. 1,760,000 yards. 609344 meters. It would take me 500 hours to swim. 20 days.

Sometimes, there are moments. Moments where I forget where I am. Forget who I am. I find that safe warm quiet place and check out for a while. The mind adapts. It protects. It distances itself from the outside world. Memories melt into general darkness just beyond the great blinkers of reality. Math games, breath games and stroke counts.

When it can.

In those moments, your body is no longer your own, but is sitting on the bottom of a pool in the deep end. Everyone above is blurry and muted. And you hold your breath.

Sober. And counting.

Wanted to detach, let go, bye bye. But the body betrays, and you stay.

You breathe.

Shattered.

Quiet. And counting.

In the desert, with dark monsters and flaming men. Naked demons and techno-sprayed-glitter-showered Unicorns. The whomp-whomp-whomp sound much like the voices do when your head is under water.

1000 miles from home.

Caught in a trap. Over and over again. Mind-splinters ripping at the seams of sanity, drowning in the deep end. But, in the deep end of a swimming pool a champagne glass doesn't break if you drop it.

And, there is no water in the desert.

The next time I left my tent was to pack it up and get in the car to go home. Shaking, shivering and scared in silence, 1000 miles from home.

ACT III - Kiss of the Dragon

"Be like water making its way through cracks. Do not be assertive, but adjust to the object, and you shall find a way around or through it. If nothing within you stays rigid, outward things will disclose themselves.

Empty your mind, be formless. Shapeless, like water. If you put water into a cup, it becomes the cup. You put water into a bottle and it becomes the bottle. You put it in a teapot, it becomes the teapot. Now, water can flow or it can crash. Be water, my friend."

~Bruce Lee

An Affair to Remember

"You can not put your hand in a bucket of water and
pull it out fast enough so that it doesn't get
at least a little bit wet."

~Don Wolff

I never shy'd away from a good affair. As Webster so
eloquently puts it, a romantic or passionate attachment of
a limited duration. That was my life. Limited, passionate
and romantic encounters... with anything. Fast and furious
was the motto.

Affairs for me weren't something that I hoped would last
until a happily ever after moment. They weren't some
princess-fantasy day-dream. I knew the reality, I knew
they were temporary. I lived the temporary, relished the
moments, no matter how brief they were and never
grieved the end.

But for some reason, there was a moment, a year, two
years maybe a little less, maybe a little more, sometime

around 2009 when I really wanted to believe. I wanted to believe in the fairy tale. I wanted to believe in the Prince. I wanted to believe there was a happily ever after out there for me. I wanted to believe in the impossible, in the magic that only Disney could weave. Then, it happened. The fairytale, the Prince Charming, the one who would slay even me to wake the princess inside. The happily ever after. The one I would never have, but even through all the promises, this Prince Charming had already kissed his princess.

He was already living his *ever after*.

But, I wanted to believe. I wanted to believe that I too could live like the princess. I wanted to believe the lie that I could have the *ever after*. The more I wanted to believe, the more lies flowed like water. I was happy with the lies. They were comfortable, like old/new skin. The lies were always there, they were safe and I happily wrapped myself in them. Drown myself in them all alone.

The Mistress kept calling. Almost as sharply as the phone ringing, a persistent nagging. She wanted her dance. She wanted her chance. She wanted her affair. It was the crux, the climax, the crescendo in music and waves which had been building.

A friendship I had treasured, abruptly ended. My job (which I was earning great money at) was stressing me out beyond belief. I had been ostracized, abandoned and cast out. My shame-cash called from the corner.

Not to mention I was starting to look and feel much older than my years.

And yet, it is almost ironic to think about, especially considering where I was. I was earning great money, doing work I liked, living in a great two bedroom place in a nice town. I had it all. I had the American Dream.

Something on the inside was broken, because everything on the outside was perfect. Born with beautiful genes and suffering with a hideous mind. Thirsting for beauty among the dry desert sands of broken lies and shattered trust. Fighting to hold it all together. There is no way to describe the fight which happens internally other than my skin is air and I am drowning inside. Scratching and fighting my very existence for a breath. Ripping through the moments of sanity trying to claw myself out. For one breath. Under perfect skin and perfect bones and perfect grades, a perfect marriage and perfect divorce, perfect employment and a perfect house with the perfect car.

To an outside observer I had achieved everything I was supposed to achieve, got the things I was supposed to get. I had put on the perfect performance. Yet, on the inside, I was unhappy. Truly, deeply and passionately unhappy.

More than just unhappy. Unsettled. Stifled and lost. I was exhausted. My soul was restless, agitated and my heart was tired. I felt like I was living a lie, and didn't even know what the lie was or where it started. I was trapped in someone else's body, breathing someone else's air, living someone else's life. The American Dream turned into my American Nightmare.

It was too much.

I had a fantasy.

I would sell everything. Pack a bag, and feign an adventure. A round-the-world, trip of a lifetime adventure of self. Everyone had read *Eat, Pray, Love* so it would be easy. I would tell one last lie. One last performance. It was a lie I desperately wanted to believe myself. A lie that I would find something *out there* to satisfy something *in here*. But lying always contains some masked truths and I had practiced and perfected the art. I was a master at creating an illusionary world around me performing with the deft expertness of an Oscar-winning Actress and convincing those close to believe the lie too. If I believed it, and I did, everyone else would too.

My lie was the adventure. I would purge everything I owned, had, gained and obtained for a year-long, or longer, adventure of the world. I started to take action before my rational mind could convince me otherwise.

I began to throw everything away. The wedding photos and graduation gowns, the memory books and mementos. The ribbons and plaques and even the little girl trophies with faux gold divers on top, it all went into the trash. My life, my death and even my breath I tried to fit in those goddamn dumpsters behind the grocery store.

I didn't want the trophies any more. I didn't want to be reminded of how well I could swim. I didn't want to hold my breath or float or blow alcoholic spit bubbles. I wanted all the didn't-wants to live-die. If someone expressed interest in one of my possessions, I gave it to them, over-enthusiastically.

My truth was to buy a plane ticket to somewhere in the world and find a nice spot somewhere to have an *accident*. I was days away from purchasing a plane ticket, but had no intention of coming back. Ever. I was planning my own death. Planning my release, my final dance, one last curtain call before landing safely into the arms of this Mistress who I had cheated so many times before and had been my nemesis for over 15 years. Yet, this same Mistress I knew would welcome me into her arms like an old lover.

It was planned in my mind. The Mistress....the Siren. I bought travel insurance so my folks wouldn't have to pay for my body to be shipped back. I made sure my life insurance policy was up to date, and I knew that no matter what, it had to look like an accident...

... because life insurance doesn't pay out for suicides.

Now the day had come. I was going to buy my one-way ticket to Asia, and start there. But there was one small, tiny, little hiccup in my plan. I didn't plan on him.

Yes. Him.

And no, this book is not about a *Him*, about how some man on a white horse came and rescued me. That is a little too cliche' for my life, and if you remember, Prince Charming NEVER saved Maleficent.

Yet, he was a curiosity. And, like a cat, I went to investigate.

He was a man I had seen at a ~~party/rave~~ "gathering" in the fall of 2004. He was a man I had exchanged glances with at the Roosevelt Hotel in Times Square of New York City in 2007 while I was there for a conference. He was a man I had never spoken to, but yet, one hot summer night in 2009 I picked him up at a strip-club and took home for a wild one-night stand. And HE just happened to be sitting in my living room six years after I first saw him.

This man and I had been secret (sometimes not so secret) long distance lovers since that wild one night stand. It had lasted for about a year, and it was an affair I relished. A secret, sordid affair. We lived 200 miles apart and would see each other about once a month to get our fix. He had no connection to my past, and didn't live in the thoughts of my future. He was free as a mustang on the plains. He was the fix of wild, crazy, unabashed, violence and passion. He was, in a word, awesome. There were no expectations, no attachments and no commitments.

There was no shame.

He is a stray comet in the infiniteness of the Universe.

His comet and my orbit met, like the Hadron Collider happening in my living room.

Every object of mass exerts a gravitational pull on every other object. In space, as well as on earth. As above, so below, as within, so without. Grave-ity increases with mass. The more massive, the greater the pull of the grave.

Gravity.
Grave.

The spiral mirroring the Milky Way, the underworld, the inner-world, our bodies, our souls, our orbits. Spinning in space. Crashing in the night sky.

Everyone has their own orbit.

Sometimes those orbits align with others and like the Earth and Moon, live in a symbiotic relationship until the end of time. A push-pull to keep appropriate distance from danger. On Ellipses. Circular. Seasonal. October.

Sometimes, orbits collide. Like gravity. Like grave-ity.

In October.

It was the space-drug of Universal proportions. In the same way some drugs can get you high, in those safe, warm and euphoric feelings. He was it. He made all the pain go away, even for just a moment. Kissing him was like kissing the creator.

It was like swimming in Teddy Bear's pocket. It was on a whim, in a gasp, in a brief moment, looking up over my laptop and in the midst of my planning, I asked:

"Do you want to come with me?"

It was the:

"Here, have a hit of something awesome and trip balls for a lifetime. The hangover will be fierce, but I promise it will be worth it" ... kind of a question.

He was never afraid of gravity.

But first, you have to understand the type of man this is. This is the man who has a hard time taking anything that someone gives to him freely. This is a man who asks no favors but will give you the shirt off of his back and stand naked and freezing in the middle of winter so that you could be warm. This is a man who should have been a millionaire six times over but is not. Even though he deserves it. He was also my killer. So, when I asked him to come with me, I never thought in a million years he would say yes.

Our lover-ship wasn't like that. It was more like the way an addict felt about getting their next fix. The weekends we were together were full of gluttonous high's, a filling of the erotic-touch-of-another-person-who-doesn't-want-a-relationship-yet-so-we-can-escape-together-in-a-safe-way tank.

And when the tanks got low, one of us would text or call the other and plan another sexy-times filled weekend.

Orbits.

It was, in fact, **THE PERFECT AFFAIR**. The perfect high. My perfect personal drug.

So when I say, I never in a million years thought he would say yes, I mean....

Never. In. A. Million.

We had talked about it before, and he had said no. He said "he didn't have the money", he said "I don't want to owe you". I counted on him saying no. I planned to walk off a cliff at the edge of the world, and I whispered... "Do you want to come with me?" My face still hidden in my laptop.

and I held my breath. One. Last. Time.

and...

He said yes.

That day, the day he said yes, that day will be seared into my brain forever.
Like the tattoo on the ankle of the tanned, toned Greek God at the edge of the pool.
Like the day I drowned clutching my soul in blood.

Like the night I had a date with pain killers and booze and prayed sleep would steal my breath.

That day, his answer changed everything.

It was late October, a time of elliptical orbits and climactic points. A time where decisions reverberate through my space with more weight than mass.

On the hardwood floors, leaf shadows danced with the sunshine streaming through the window. Earth's breath of breeze whispering blindly. I don't known how much of a person's soul is visible to most people, but he saw mine through words. My body just hanging loosely like a gangly covering taking up space. A painter once said the body is most beautiful, and telling, at the joints: the shoulders, neck, elbows, wrists, hips, knees and ankles. We are all glued together, and I was coming undone.

The morning had greeted us with sun and silence, hand holding and a walk to the french bakery just a few blocks away. We had casual conversation over gourmet coffee and freshly baked pastries. Elephants hidden under rugs, lovely interludes lie layering over uneasiness. He was light. He was the Sun. He was soft and gentle. His arms around me smoothed the edges of life which grated against my soul. My marrow. The deepest parts of me were stars in the field of his body. The rings around his Saturn. Orbits in the space-time of infiniteness.

If time is the soul of the world, then this moment must be somewhere.

This moment breathes.

This moment lives forever.

See, this man isn't just a man. He is a professional. A former professional bodyguard, which means he was paid BIG BUCKS to make sure that accidents DIDN'T happen. He was NOT the kind of bodyguard that escorted celebrities to their cars, he was NOT the kind of bodyguard that stood by the door and frisked people coming into a meeting. He wasn't even the kind that The Russian would hire. No, he was a real, honest-to-goodness, Man-On-Fire, *Blackwater*-type, stabbed, shot, beaten, drowned, smuggling, protected-unnamed-officials-from-mexican-cartel-assassinations, off-the-grid, fly-in-unmarked-private-jets, nameless-faceless-multiple-passport, mercenary-type bodyguard. He didn't just *know* the Mistress of Death, he slept with her, ate with her, danced with her, loved her, tasted the deepest parts of her and did her bidding like the perfectly good puppy of a Mistress does. He scared me. Scared me in the deepest parts of my soul which made me feel a little bit funny. He scared me because he was strong.

So strong.

Grave strong.

He was the only man I met who could match my strength of will. Match my strength in determination and defiance, and match my intimate knowledge of the Mistress of Death. He was my killer, my murderer and I hoped, he could match my fear.

Perhaps he scared me the most when he said yes from across the room. Scared me when, in some secret alternate Universe, he looked the Mistress of Death right in the eye and said No.

Yes.
and No.

A mere mortal who has the soul-level strength and could look deep into the eyes of the Mistress of Death, the woman who he did bidding for, and tell her she was just going to have to wait. To tell her to Fuck. Off. For a long, long time. A mere mortal with with the strength and power of the Gods. The power to protect me from the most dangerous thing on the planet.....

Myself.

He didn't slay dragons, no. He made those dragons his pet. I was Malificent, and I had finally met my match.

Hell didn't stand a chance.

This is what my truth looks like.

For the first time in as long as I could remember, I could breathe. I could do more than just gasp. I didn't have to compete, I didn't have to lie, I didn't have to drink or fuck or swim in ice-cold oceans or run screaming naked through the desert to get high. I didn't have to hold my breath, count or do anything but just.
Be.
Me.

I sat there, and clicked.

Lost

"... And when everything else is gone,
you can be rich in loss."

~**Rebecca Solnit**

I lost a lot of friends over the years. Some through choice, but most not my own. Friendships which were deep, truth, lifelines of sanity in my otherwise crazy shatter-filled life.

The lifelines.

The loss felt like the ripping of sails on the deep ocean of my heart, resonating through space with the rumble of a deep baritone.

My dad was a baritone, a deep clear voice which could be heard as a strong stabilizing force from the choir pit at church on Sunday. *Amazing Grace* and deep despair breathing in the same sanctuary. His voice rang true from the pulpit as only an Elder does as the collection plate is passed. There were so many Sundays, dressed in my best Sunday clothes, sitting on the hard pine benches, looking at my shoes, counting down the minutes and wondering...

How many others want to scream out right now?

And I would sit. Silent. Lost amongst the sheep. Sheep. People. The Sheeple. What is the rod and staff? And why don't I feel comforted sitting here? All of the silent people searching for a connection. A soul-to-soul meeting with God.

I prayed. Prayed for swim meets on Sunday so I didn't have to sit un-comforted in church. Prayed for some all-knowing, all-being, all-forgiving, all-merciful, all-justifying Santa Claus in the sky to come and do something.

Prayed.

And nothing happened. No strike, no forgiveness, no joy in my heart, just a constant baritone voice from the choir.

So I held my breath. When everyone else would pray, I would see how long I could hold my breath. I played breath games. I held still. Even the atoms against my skin stopped moving. I wanted to get high. I wanted that ecstatic experience, but it never came. I held my breath during the dunking of the baptismal waters, and yet there was no jolt, no electricity, no nothing. I wasn't even under the surface for more than a brief second.

How is that baptismal? I didn't feel anything happen. All the Sunday School stories and things people have said was that, now because of a quick dunking of the water I was *saved*. But, shouldn't *saved* go along with a feeling? A jolt? An epiphany?

Baptism is just another form of an initiatory rite and humans have long since pursued this feeling. From the ancient Egyptians, to the Knights Templar, the Masons to the born again Fundamentalists. But, why water? Is it just to swim in that amniotic fluid again for a brief moment? Is it due to it's conductivity of light and energy? Is it because of some unity or oneness which happens when you are in it?

Yes.

What does *being saved* truly feel like?

I don't know.

There was a moment one day, in the grass behind God's house, a moment above all others I wished for saving. A moment of clarity in the black-zombie-ness of *after*. After the blood, after the hospital, but before death. After the splash, but before the deep. I wanted to be touched. Touched in a non-violent way. I needed to be hugged and helped and held against the monsters of my skin. I could still feel the predatory hands around my neck. The memory still stalking my days. The pixilating ghost hands were always there and it was hard to breathe.

My mother went with me to the hospital. Spoke with the doctor like I wasn't in the room and somehow, someway, I ended up in the grass behind God's house. I was a 15-year-old girl voice sitting in front of my father. The Elder. His voice of Amazing Grace, mine squeaky like a mouse. He was the son of the woman I loved more than anything. The man who had kept me safe from the boogie-men. The man who taught me how to shoot a bow and arrow and laughed like chimes on a summer breeze. Wanting to spill everything, wanting it all to come out of me like some verbal vomit. Expunging the poison like rotten food of the flesh.

I was just a girl whose voice didn't work. My mouth felt like it had been stuffed with cotton. Choking and sputtering, trying to breathe.

Just breathe.

The only thing I could get to come out was...

"Dad, I had sex."

Thinking. Judging. Ashamed.

A slight movement back, away from me, like the boils of black death were starting to show on my skin.

"What did I do wrong" he said.

"How did I fail you?" he said.

An ocean of space appeared before us. Silence would have been better than the perfect storm of word waves which crashed into my ears. I wanted to tell him. I did. I wanted to tell him the whole story, from the very beginning. I tried... I tried... I think I tried... but he just seemed to be getting further and further away. My words weren't coming. My father, who, once so close, was getting sucked out into an ocean of space right before my eyes. Getting smaller and smaller. Blackness invading, my eyes narrowing trying to keep his face into focus, trying to stay with him.

But, he is so far away.

I wanted to tell him. But, I never got that far with words. … and, I don't remember what happened after that.

Alone, I made my own prescription. A plan to counteract the violation. A plan to know the pleasure of touch. Any pleasure, no matter how painful.

We are islands, singular organisms searching for connection and swinging wildly. Deep desires for solitary silence and overwhelming cravings for a deep connection.

Maybe I was the one who got sucked out into space that day. My broken body of earth, thousands and thousands of miles away.

Someday. I thought.

Someday. Someone will find my bones held together by sand and heat in this god-forsaken deserted place, and they will hold them. They will put them back together.

Someday.

I cheer those I have lost and have deep realizations for just how short our little lives are. People are stretched for time running out quicker and quicker each day. They live in their hurried world, not paying attention until it ruins their routine. Does the **saving** feel like connection?

These questions came by the thousands over the years, swimming around in my head like lost little faith-fish. Arguments and ideas tend to be bolstered by history and sociology degrees, a savvy business sense and evolutionary tendencies. Yet the question remains, what are we really being saved from? If not just ourselves?

There is a lot of money changing hands in this saving business, and I can't rightly believe that it would be as easy as hitting the little save button on the file menu. The truth is, no one is going to save you. Just like no one saved me.

The truth is, you have to make the choice to save yourself.

I quit swimming the year on the grass behind God's house. I never entered the water again to train. I never put the suit and cap and goggles and listened to the beep from the blocks. It wasn't in this big performance of ...

"I Quit!"

I just stopped going to practice. Stopped going one day in the blue.

But the questions have always stayed with me. Questions which were revisited on the many sleepless nights which plague me. Questions to which I have drawn a conclusions:

Heaven and Hell exist where you want them to, whether it is some far off distant place above or below you, or you are living in the moment. It all exists because you believe it does. God exists because you believe he does. Belief is powerful. But as powerful as belief is, it doesn't make things true.

Belief in those moments kept me flying. Belief kept me breathing, yet I knew, intimately that being saved is more reinforcement of this idea that there is a victim and the saving is coming from an outside force to intervene and make things better. I think in this fantastic way, fundamentalists are exactly the same as new-age healers. We are all born again in some way. I mean, Anne Rice was even born again into Catholicism and yet, left the church AGAIN. I think the truth exists somewhere in the middle of these extremes.

The truth is, we are just little drops of water walking around on a giant rock, floating through infinite space, in elliptical orbit.

The truth for me was that I craved, desired and needed to feel the ecstatic merging. I wanted the enlightened experience. The connection with something outside of myself so true and intense it felt like it was living inside of me all along. I wanted that universal touch upon my brow. The merging into the oneness of everything. The holy nirvana. As such a solitary creature, I craved the touch. Panted with wanton breath for it. Pursued this ecstatic celebration of heaven on earth with the desire of a addict wanting their next hit.

I did feel it, and not just through the death experience, but through the life experience. There are those very few times, unassisted with drugs or booze or religious fervor. The point between two ends where magic happened. Those points were fleeting though, and like a high of any other kind, they didn't last forever, and the lows always followed. A balance per se. An even-ing. A yin to the yang, light to the dark, in to the out. A dry to the wet.

There was always water.

Everyone searches for their drug. Everyone searches for their own personal moments of ecstasy, of connection, of *God's blessing* like another hit. It is that touching of those moments which make us all addicts. Fundamentalist Christian or Buddhist seeking enlightenment, Gnostic or Atheist, Hindu or Creationist, we all search our little lives for those moments of happiness and joy.

But, like an addict, when we find it, that thing which brings us joy, the thing which warms our heart and makes us feel alive - we don't ever want to let go. We are all addicts. We all collect something, and at some point, we lose it. Then, we are rich in loss.

Michelle Williams once spoke candidly about the loss of Heath Ledger.

"...The 'rich in loss' made me laugh. I would just think, 'Filthy stinking rich! Filthy stinking rich!' in a perverse-gallows-humor kind of way. It made me laugh, it made me feel drunk, it made me feel high with loss, in that tightrope kind of way of sadness and hysteria. And when you don't have ideas like that, it feels too messy to bear. It gave me great comfort. It was something I would repeat to myself, like a mantra. Because for some time it felt like we had lost everything. And those words, that idea, calmed me down."

I wanted the calm, and got the loss. I lost it all. I get it now.

Hundreds and thousands and millions of losses over the years. Little pin-pricks wanting to bleed me dry. Most of the loss my own fault, just shattered remnants of circumstance and incorrect assumption. But all reflections of the state I was in at the time that I made them.

Let me say that part again - reflections of the mental, emotional, physical and spiritual state I was in. External reflections of self. My water looking back at me. The outside to my inside. If you ever want to gauge where you are in life, just look at what you surround yourself with. The type of people. The things. Look at the circumstances. Then take a real good look, have a real close heart to heart with why you keep the company you do. These reflections can be heartbreaking and exhilarating all in the same breath, especially when you lose it.

When you lose it all, the truth becomes clear.

The First Hit.

The human brain logs, retains and remembers everything it sees, feels and experiences. It is just the recalling process which is, quite frankly, the problem.

I never learned how to vocalize my internal pain. I never learned how to talk. Sure, I talked. I talked a lot. Gregarious, outgoing, sociable, pleasant. But, I was also a competitive swimmer, and if you talk to anyone who has swam competitively for years, you will soon understand that there is a lot going on under the surface.

It is quiet once you are insulated in the wet.

Swimmers are an astonishing mental bunch. Comforted in their own thoughts with the sounds of water and breath and bubbles and splashing. It is easy to get lost when you are swimming. The body is trained, the muscles have memory, and there are points of lucidity lost in the molecules of hydrogen and oxygen. I could easily swim 600 meters before even waking up in the morning. Just like it is so easy to get lost, it is just as easy to get disoriented. Yes, you stare at the black T-shaped tiles on the bottom of the pool, day in and day out. But, muscle memory will take over and you can easily check out, go into auto-pilot, and do everything right, still while mentally gone. Over the years, I memorized the landmarks in my pool. Exactly where the jets were, the flags hung, the stairs. I memorized where the chips in the paint at the bottom of the pool were and would track the growth of chipping away day by day as I stared at it, going back and forth and back again. I knew how many strokes were between each point. I knew the breath count and could track speed and time by those watermarks. It is a calm disorientation process, and somewhere in the middle of it all, I could easily lose the plot... and pick it up again just as easily.

Yes, you see, swimmers, *real swimmers* are all in need of an escape in the water. There is something refreshingly calm about it. Head buried just under the surface. The water doesn't care how old you are, how many awards you have won, how much money you make, it just wants you to be in it. It doesn't critique, it doesn't abandon, it doesn't need anything but you. It doesn't care how many people you have slept with, what scars you carry or how you carry them.

It just needs you.

On the same and yet ironically other hand, swimmers also have quite the reputation to be heavy drinkers/drug users and many suffer from eating disorders. We are the broken minds of athletics. The ones who don't count on a teammate, can do everything for ourselves, can out-drink our friends till 4 a.m. and still show up at 6 a.m. for practice. I would dare you to ask even the best in the sport, Michael Phelps, Janet Evans, Mark Spitz or Dana Torres, but they would all tell you the same thing:

Swimming is as much mental as it is physical.

And, swimming gets you high. Just like the ability to easily check out during practice, the highness comes before a race. Right before a race I was always sick to my stomach with anxiety. Thinking about the times that are needed, the fine motor movement that is required, the stretching and hot shower and shaving and tapering. Even after years of competing, every big race, every performance and every self-imposed expectation is marked by a big adrenaline surge. It is the adrenaline surge in the body and brain that is the addiction. The stress the mental-ists place upon themselves to psych up. But it is that addiction, that high, that nauseating, singular-focused mental-activity which brings a lifetime of cravings.

Cravings.

My internal secret need to get my fix. A fix that I have been chasing.

For years.

I didn't talk about the first time my brain experienced the euphoric and ecstatic high of dying. I didn't talk about the bloody vampiric initiation or about the Novocain of booze and drugs and men. I never spoke of the secret society, the girls or the married men. You don't speak underwater. You can rage and scream and smile and laugh and no one can see behind the cap and goggles. And you can cry. You can cry and sob and yet... There is nothing to give you away under the wake of water off your skin. Under the water where no one can see, it is a secret world of self. This talent to endure was nothing more than an innocent ignorance of an alternative...

I wear a good fearless face on land.

Fearless face.... like a cowardly lion. I was the Cowardly Lion in my very first performance.
The one in the *Wizard of Oz*, in fourth grade. It was the first and only time I got a 4.0. Straight A's. A perfect young coward with a fearless face. I had tried out for the part of Dorothy, I sang my little rainbow heart out, but, a cute little blond with perky blue eyes was Dorothy, of course. I was a brown-haired, brown-eyed make-up

coated, teddy-bear fuzz covered lion. A fearless face. As perfect as my fuzz covered performance was, I never forgot my humanness. I never forgot for one moment that I was NOT a lion.

Performances are funny that way though... if you commit to the character long enough, sometimes you forget what is real.

Murder Creeps from the Cracks

"Most of these women don't really want to die,
they want to kill the pain."

~Charlotte Davis Kaslo

I could feel the killing thing inside of him, in the midst of the darkness, pumping music, naked women dancing and the dollar bills floating through the air. I could hear it. I could hear the Mistress of Death singing on his arm and I loved him from the moment I first saw him... just for that. I knew what death in overworked hands felt like. It felt like 15-year-old shame and shattered trust. It felt like the Killing Fields and Austowitz's locked inside my rib house. It was the shadows and dark places which hid in the folds of the grey matter heart of my skull. It was in him, on him and all around him.

The Mistress of Death, sitting on his face.

I locked eyes with him and wanted him.

I wanted to fuck-kill him. I wanted him to fuck-kill me. I wanted to push and thrash and rail and slam my body all over his death hands. And we did. Murdering each other over and over again with our bodies. Murdering me with his shiv. Shredding him with my vampiric teeth and claws.

I wanted his hands of death inside of me. I know there is a trigger in there somewhere, I know I can find it. I deserve to find it. I wanted him to kill the things of me I couldn't reach inside and kill myself. I wanted him to murder those things inside of me that I couldn't touch. I wanted him to kill the fear, murder the panic, and slay the anger. He will do it, then I will be right, then I will win and my anger will have vengeance.

But, I am wrong.

He could reach inside. With his strong hands of death.

His death hands with a choke-hold on all the bad and cruel and shame and lust of the world trapped inside a woman-girl.

He lived in a house of taint and darkness, of fire-breathing dragons and Bruce Lee brothers. Of life and death and everything that screamed strength in a world of man. The Dragon-Man. Strength without the need for constant dominance. He was a King, without ever needing to wave a flag of proclamation.

It was in this man-ness, this lust and fuck-killing, that when he reached in, he almost drowned in the blood-secrets. Tore my insides onto my outsides until there was nothing left. Water and blood and snot and drool, piss and vomit and secrets spilled out on the floor of our little fuck-kill palace. Like a horrible little aborted bastard child. Guts and blood and pain and pain and pain spraying him.

And him,
calmly wiping his eyes.

Reaching in again and saying yes. Holding me.

And, for the first time in my life, I was safe on land. Not hiding under the wet, insulated by the water and blood and piss and guts, untouchable by the touches.

I was safe and finally alive in the arms of a man who murdered me. I lived in his death grip, breathed in his soul-slaying and moved into his life.

<u>Truth Tripping</u>

Gamble everything for love. . . .
Half-heartedness doesn't reach into majesty.
You set out to find God,
but then you keep stopping for long periods
at mean-spirited road houses.
Don't wait any longer.
Dive in the ocean,
leave and let the sea be you. . . .

-RUMI, from Say I Am You

As competitive swimmers get older, we seek out the solitude of the pool. We like to go when the pool is empty and we don't have to share a lane. I have noticed, retired competitive swimmers do not like sharing lanes too much. We like to stretch and expand and watch the tiles go by in mindless patterns. We don't want to have to think about the space available for arms as we pass, circle swimming or even talking. We just want to go, claim our little piece of watery universe and only when we are done, will we briefly nod to our neighbor.

Who... nods back, and our communication commences in some unspoken language of respect and solitude.

Yet, even in this solitude of tile-gazing and flip-turns, over all these years I always swam with someone else. I always traveled with the darkness. The Mistress of Death never left my side.

I left the country in January of 2011 with no plans to come back. I left everything behind except for her. I took her traveling with me traveling the world. Five months overseas and out there. Five months going through third-world countries, eating third-world food and going to the bathroom in third-world toilets. Five months traveling over 20,000 miles. Showers were not much more than hand-held heads above a toilet and the drinking and tooth-brushing water was always bottled. It wasn't in some *Eat, Pray, Love* search for soul, although that was the excuse/lie/whatever-you-want-to-call-it. No, it was me, the Dragon-man and the Mistress of Death, all traveling together. All looking for an escape, and it was glorious.

Not once did I think about what was going to happen next. Not once did I make a plan beyond that day. I just lived in the moment. Alone, and yet kept company with the *him* and the *her*. A menage-a-trois of chaos.

Alone.

Creeping with Chaos.

The first hit of this journey, of this running, of this adventure with the Mistress of Death, the Dragon-man and me was in front of the airport in the middle of Saigon at 4 a.m. After traveling for close to 24 hours. There was nothing to go back to, there was nothing left waiting for me at home. Nothing left for me to hold on to. There were no more attachments or expectations. I was not going back.

And I still wasn't quite sure how I was going to do anything, if I were to do anything. He was always there. There was never a moment where I was truly alone.

Ever.

The Mistress of Death was there, he was there, but... I didn't feel suffocated. I wasn't drowning or gasping or running or anything.... I was just being. If two is company, three was definitely a crowd, yet I didn't feel too crowded.

We ran and ran, rock-star'd and bull-rushed our way through customs of five countries in three days. After finally landing in Saigon at 4 a.m. after a perilous customs transition through an unnamed Chinese airport. (For the record, Saigon/Ho Chi Minh City is not the most friendly place in the world at 4 a.m. after traveling 24+ hours.)

As much as this book really isn't about my travels, in a very real and parallel sense, it is.

In just the first few hours of **Welcome to Asia** there were cockroaches the size of my fist crawling all over my backpack. We had stopped wandering around the Vietnamese streets looking for an open Hostel at 4 a.m., I think more from exhaustion than anything else. But stopped none-the-less for a bit of Pho. It was as if all the cockroaches in Asia wanted to welcome us because as soon as we set down our bags they were all over it. The second day (after a few hours of sleep) we found ourselves face-to-face with the underground (or in most cases, sidewalk sale) sex trade. Companion bars and lovely ladies offering their hand, a bit of conversation, and some flesh for a dollar. Only in this land, these ladies where sadly not self-proprietors. The madam's stalked the corners like hungry lions keeping a tight leash on their meat. In Vietnam, we stayed four days.

For just a brief moment in Vietnam, when I stood still for just one second, I stood on the rooftops of restaurants and imagined the helicopters leaving on that ominous day in the 70's. I saw statues of Quan Yin riding dragons and reaching out in compassion just as I wished that God would just reach his hand down and pick me up from those rooftops. Wished to be taken away to this heavenly place of all the joy and peace and nirvana that I was promised as a kid in Sunday School. I wished that all the pain and anger and hurt and everything dark in my little soul-world would disappear.

But, yet, no hand of God. No magical pill. No nirvanic experience. Just standing in a brief moment contemplating history and space and time and orbits and God and darkness .... once again. Under the watchful eye of Quan Yin, holding the hand of the Mistress of Death and her henchman.

Pictures, check. Pho, check. Bombed-out buildings next to five-star hotels, check. Vietnam was done. On a bathroom-less bus run, a bit more and cross the border into the Kingdom of Cambodia. No security check, no TSA, nothing more than a little bribe to the bus driver/customs agent at the border (with included potty-stop and fried tarantula feast), a cute little sticker on our passports and we were off again....

We got lost in Phnom Penh, and finally found our lovely guest house fit for dragons and dreams and stopped moving for longer than an hour. It was when we stopped for a breath, something happened. Somewhere squished in the very middle of the journey. Squished between Chinese New Year and Valentines Day, in a country squished between Vietnam and Thailand, Cambodia changed everything.

If you have never been to Cambodia, it is the paradox of everything good and evil in this world. A lovely, beautiful, tragic, heartbreaking, feast for the senses. Every day, in every single way. I found this charming little tidbit out when I stopped moving long enough and started looking at my surroundings. Cambodia is a country in which the United States carpet bombed, secretly, for five full years after the official end of the Vietnam War. Cambodia was a nation of people caught in an international conflict and suffered tremendously for it. One quarter of the population of Cambodia (almost two million people) were decimated through the holocaust and genocidal practices of the Khmer Rouge. If the Mistress of Death had a home base anywhere, she was happiest in Cambodia. She gluttonously collected millions of souls through starvation, war and murder between 1975 and 1979. Ending only the same year I was born. And that day, the day over 30 years after the end of the war, the day when I stepped off the bus and placed my foot on the Cambodian soil, I thought I would go deaf from the ghost screams carried on the wind. It was dusty, dry, and flat. The blood-stained earth was infectious and I felt as though with one step I had walked off the edge of the world.

Off the edge of the world and directly into my own soul.

The people, the people effected me the most. They were poor. No, not poor. They were destitute. I had more money in my pocket walking off that bus than most of them made in a lifetime. But... but, these people were happy. Truly, deeply, soul-level happy. Welcoming, hugging, shaking hands, looking at you in the eye and asking questions about everything in your life.

They had one things I couldn't touch. There was no amount of money which could purchase the joy they carried.

There were a few basic questions that every single person you met would ask, in one hurried breath, with no time for you to answer before you were cut-off with the next question:

What is your name?
Where are you from?
How old are you?
Do you know President Obama?
His wife's name is Michelle, he was born in Hawaii.
I love President Obama!

They would exclaim. Then, without a breath, an obligatory:

Do you want _____ (a postcard/necklace/t-shirt/juice/fruit/water/tuktukride or to give me a dollar)?

They were welcoming like nothing I had ever experienced. How? I wondered. I had every-THING in life that they didn't, and yet, they were truly happy. Happier in a moment than I had every been in my whole life. They were living in one of the most horrifically decimated places in the world. So decimated in fact, that to find a native Cambodian resident over the age of 55 is like finding the Ark of the Covenant itself.

Cambodia was the paradox of my soul which had now climaxed into physicality. It was weird. Every day my feet touched the Cambodian earth, my dark soul screamed in orgasmic pain/pleasure. It was as if some dark Sado-Masochistic fantasy was manifesting in my aura.

So, I started to watch. I started to embrace quiet on land, to walk softer, to listen a little more and feel the world that was beginning to bloom in my hands. I started to enjoy this painful process. These people didn't care what I did, how much money I made, what job defined me and my life. They didn't have expectations or a form to fit into, they just wanted to know about me. They wanted to know the answers to significant, personal and sometimes intimate questions. It was such a dichotomy. Killing Fields and Ancient Holy sites of prayer and reverence. Sharing the same earth. Sharing the same blood. Love and Death, Life and Indifference, married.

It was everything.

In Cambodia, there was a darkness that pulls everything in. The rage, the anger, the sadness, the impossibilities. Just sucking and sucking and sucking until one day. One day silently among the stars. One day in a moment of the blackest black, and tears and emotions and emptiness and Killing fields and Temples, It explodes.

Explodes into brilliance.

Explodes into light.

Explodes into color and glitter and Universes and Life and...

.... and Breath.

One day, a day like any other. A day where a small trip on the back of a motorbike brought me face to face with a ten foot glass cylindrical column filled with skulls.

The sucking sound.

A day where in a desperate attempt to get away from the sadness and killing. To get away from the darkness and slaying. Trying to run from the blackness and looking through tear stained eyes and taking a wrong turn, I end upon the wrong side of a hill in front of a Temple. A Temple hidden between shanties of a small village of people who spoke no English. A Temple whose 12-foot walls are filled with sacred paintings of Buddha and inlayed with gold and jewels. A Temple where the floor is layer upon layer of handwoven rugs, and ornate wooden columns supporting silk tapestries. A Temple where villagers are taking off my shoes, hugging and hand holding and escorting me to the shrine, and not speaking a word. Just smiling. In the shanties of a Cambodian village lived a Temple where a Buddhist Abbott has come to bless the villagers with Jasmine Water and blessing-filled bracelets only once a year. That day. That hour. That wrong turn. A Temple of the Blessed. A Temple where there was peace. There was perfection, calm and everything was good in the eye of the storm. Perfect.

There was air.

An explosion of air.

I was stunned.

Stunned and overcome with emotions. Waves upon crashing waves of emotion. Tear-stained and exhausted. Everything I had drown in, drained with each tear. Leaving in the wet was everything I was and knew and expected myself to be. Shedding and shedding and shedding tear by tear upon the thread-bare and colorful rugs beneath my knees, head hanging and weeping water. In front of strangers who just smiled and hugged.

Weeping the water I had collected for years. Weeping the water I had drown in. Weeping and weeping and weeping, watching the puddles collect at my knees and watching my own reflection on the watery skin. The water I spent so many years drowning in, now slowing staining the thread colors dark under my rough knobby kneed skin. It was gone.

It was all gone.

And when the water was gone, I just sat. Motionless. Silent. Suspended in time. Suspended in timelessness. In blackness and now-ness and everything-ness and nothing-ness. In gold and color and beauty and grace. In the middle of the third-world country that is Cambodia.

There was silence. And when it was quiet, and I no longer had to shut my eyes and cover my ears to the world.

There was acceptance.
There was life.

There was breath.

Drenched and smelling of jasmine and blessings, drowned and smiling. Happy. And happiness looks a little bit different when tried on people like me. Cambodia changes something on the inside of a person. It touched something deep. It slid into those dark little cracks and breathed life between the rocks.

She Speaks.

"There is only one God...
.... and his name is Death.
... and there is only one thing we say to Death.
... Not Today."

You cannot converse with death, no...

Death only speaks, and you shall only listen. That was my problem. I needed to listen, because when The Mistress of Death spoke, she held the hand of the Dragon-man and whispered in my ear. This is what she said:

"I have been called many names throughout time. From the dawn of light itself, I have existed. I am the shadow, the killer, the mercenary and the merciful. I am Male and Female, Santa Muerte and Lilith herself.

I am Death.

I am loved, hated, celebrated and cursed.

I am the Mistress and the Guardian, God and the essence of Universe.

You have these grand ideas of me, from very beautiful and seductive to red scales and horns. But, let the record show, I am magnificently adorned in your lies. Loathed, Feared. Embraced. I am the only thing which exists even after everything else ceases.

I teach you about life, love, appreciation, gratitude and humility. I reflect to you, your fragile state, impermanence and ignorance. I celebrate the moment you are born, knowing that eventually you will end up in my embrace.

I touch everyone. And, every Thing.

I am infectious and seductive, celebrated and seeked. I take from you your most beloved and give you respite from suffering. And yet, my most powerful weapon is my ability to seduce you to do my bidding. I am a Magician, master and Artist. I create with your diseased, discarded and bone-ridden beauty.

And yet, there is always a point in which I ask each living human:

"What is your price?

"What is more precious than life? Presuming a persons life is worth living?"

"What do you value the most? What if I took everything away, what would you be left with? That is what I want. It is the price I ask in exchange for your breath.

If it was your wife? gone. Your money and retirement? vanished. Peace and love? I took that too. What is left? What is that secret thing?

There, yes that.
That is what I want. That is my price for your life."

"Would you rather forget?
No?
Then I will make you forget again and again and again."

"So then, I ask again, What is your price?"

"That dusty abandoned thing over there in the corner? Is that the reason you live?"

"Then why the hell aren't you living like it is?"

… and Death reminds us to live.

In the Pulitzer Prize winning book, The Denial of Death, Ernest Becker speaks of death when he says:

" ...the idea of death, the fear of it, haunts the human animal like nothing else; it is a mainspring of human activity--activity designed largely to avoid the fatality of death, to overcome it by denying in some way that it is the final destiny for man."

… And Death responds,

"My dear little human, I am so much more. I am Le Petite Mort, Enlightenment, and Ecstasy. Deep and wide, baby, deep and wide. You love me baby, and you hate yourself for that.

... and oh, I love you too! I love you enough to do my bidding for me. To hold me in your hands and squeeze, squeeze hard, harder than anything you have ever squeezed in your life. Squeeze until your hands bleed.

Then, take comfort. Comfort in the belief that I am a warm blanket. A blanket stitched with gilded 'Hail Marys' and platinum seams of 'You are Healed'.

but, sometimes, you crack...

Crack like the 'I regret nothing I've done, of the lives I've taken. It wasn't by some spiritual awakening, or by religious rebirth. It was by my knowing, intimately knowing, life is too short. Like in some strange way, it is as if the lives I've saved more than make up for the losses.' And yet you have guilt gorilla's smashing around on your insides.

Talk about a bull in the China shop, pfffft.

I mean, I understand, it is very difficult to deal with that God over there, That god of War. He is so horrifically brutal sometimes. The blood, misery and utter stupidity of it all. It's always the same, you know; the screams, the pain, the illness that follows, the starvation. And it's always the innocents who suffer the most. Most of these souls are grateful for my arrival. I am the end to the pain and the suffering.

After all, I am their relief.
They call for me. You see, I can't stop. Like a bloodlust vampire, they call to me, from their soul, to mine.

I am the emotion of a steel driven snowflake.

What do I mean to you?

I am a large collection of individual pieces. Like a trapped growing organism. Individual ideas assimilated into a larger scope of beautiful deadly work."

"Look for the beauty in death and it will seduce you. The growth, acceptance and surrender to the divinely inevitable. Live the legacy, it is only through death could each person be so much more, in more relationships, in deeper and stronger relationships."

It has been said that we are not truly prepared to live until we are prepared to die. Life assumes a greater meaning and purpose when we fully appreciate the fact we are going to die. Our death is real and will be marked by a specific day on the calendar. All the days leading up to that one assume a special significance. Time passes so quickly. When we prepare to live with the full knowledge that we will die, we stop taking life and the people we love for granted. Our own lives, and our significant relationships, become authentic.

"I lead you wandering blind towards a cliff. None of us know which step it will be that will cause us to fall, we only are certain of one thing - that we are getting closer to the edge. Once we are over the edge, we can never get back. Such is life, and such is the fact that we will meet one day.

You can do it, I believe in you."

Everyone can learn something, and not necessarily anything; from the phenomenon of birth; but from death we can learn everything. It is that little transition in between which means the most.

"There is only one God...
.... and his name is Death."

I finally realized. I wasn't chasing some ecstatic merging with God swatting the Mistress of Death away from me like a persistent mosquito, I was chasing death herself. I was craving the Life-experience through the Death-experience and running from it all at the same time. But the truth is:

I am the Mistress.

I hold Death, and I am God.

The Cliffs

"I lead you wandering blind towards a cliff, closer and closer to the edge with each step...."

~ Mistress of Death

After a month of heart-whipping and soul-solicitousness in Cambodia, I moved into Thailand. It was time for recovery and a good place to bury my head in the sand and my body in the waves. Thirty days of nothing but Thai beer, Thai beaches, coconuts and untying the brain-bending. Thirty days goes fast when the days are spent under the sun by the ocean (or private pool), and the nights are restaurant eating and beer drinking. Although, I do remember one particular week being on Tsunami alert, waiting to hear sirens, waiting to evacuate. But apparently the flooding of Thailand would happen a year or so after Japan's coast was toast. Done by heavy rains and not Tsunami's.

My body of destructive water had nothing on Mother Nature.

After recovering a bit in Thailand, I blindly headed south across the equator. South to where the water moves backwards and south into Bali, Indonesia.

Bali. The Island of the Gods.

In the 15 years of running and five months of traveling, I finally got to my climactic point. My climactic point of frustrating agony and battle between life vs. death, god vs. man, air vs. water and everything bloody, broken and in-between.

I had left everything I owned in the garbage, everything but a 40lb backpack of bare necessities, traveling through seven countries, and logging more than 20,000 miles.

It was hard. There were a thousand and one times in which I thought to myself :

"I am crazy, I have officially lost my mind, I just want to go home and crawl into my warm bed and be around all my safe stuff."

But the problem was, all that stuff was gone.....everything I owned in the world was sitting inside my backpack. But what I realized was:

I was traveling with much more baggage than just a backpack.

Everything in my life was culminating. To travel as far away on the globe as possible, for the Universe to conspire to get me to that point.

Conspire through rave-raids, busted-up border crossings, and real-life GI Joes. Conspire through back-splatter radiations stations, cockroach kamikaze attacks and bombed out buildings in Vietnam. Conspire through Cambodian deep fried tarantula's, a boarder war and Thai beaches. Everything in my little Universe conspired so perfectly that I was standing on the edge of a cliff at the end of the world in Bali. Standing on the edge of a cliff after a hair-raising motorcycle adventure through Third-world gridlock on a scooter. After a mile hike through a jungle with monkeys that want to eat your brains like murderous little hair covered zombies.

That kind of conspire.

It all finally made sense. It all made sense on the perilous cliffs of Bali.

I saw the cliffs and knew it was time.

It took just a moment, not even a split second, to throw everything off that cliff. Everything and everything and everything else off of that damn damn cliff. The emotions and expectations, thoughts and ideas of what *should* happen.

Everything.

Everything those murderous hands of Death's henchman pulled out of me. Diving off that damn cliff. Diving into all the crashing sounds of those shame waves.

From one hundred fifty feet above the crashing on the rocks into the clearness and into the yes. Sitting there, dangling my feet over the edge, between the devil and the deep blue sea. So what did I do? I grabbed the Mistress of Death and threw her to her very own demise. Throwing her off the damned death cliff.

There was nothing but air.

Air is all around us, it keeps everything on this planet alive. Yet, we only see it when it is polluted, only really pay attention to it when it is unavailable. It is invaluable yet invisible. Necessary yet elusive. It moves us, carries our words and yet we cannot see, hear or feel it until it is no longer available. Just ask someone to describe air to you. You will begin to see.

It was as if those rocks could really stop the waves.

Thoughts and expectations went into the deep blue. Glamour and success went swimming with the fishies. Houses and cars and lakes and boats, the symphony, the Irish, and the bikers. Froth and sand and cool wet spray. My body shook, and my mind went black into a deep deep hole of space and time. Stolen seconds at the very end before the velvet. In that moment, the waves of land crashed onto the water and my legs were dangling over the edge. There were no ropes, no fence, no chain to keep me back. My feet and legs flirting with the deep blue of space death crashing a hundred fifty feet below.

This was it. My moment. I wanted the air as desperately as I had wanted it when I was trapped under water. I desired it and nothing else. Jumping, falling, flailing, floating. The images moved through my mind like smoke. I wouldn't scream, I wouldn't make a sound, I would just let go. I would slip, and embrace the rocks below at close to 80 miles an hour. That should do it. Yes. We are ready. The death cliff and I.

I was at peace with this decision, and I was ready.

On the count of three...

One...

Two...

"Smile!"

It was the deep voice of my dragon-coated ***deus ex machina*** I had left lost in the jungle with the fur-zombies. I looked up, and time stopped as the camera snapped. It is forever captured, a picture of my freedom. A moment of raw, pure, life. With tears and smiles, instead of rocks, crashing upon my face with the water.

** ** ** **

Five hundred million years ago, organisms lived in the ocean. The fossils of their single-cell-ness tell us stories of age in the deep blueness of the sea. *Fossil*, in Welsh, meaning bed.

Grave.
Gravity.

Oceanic grave-beds.

Skeletons in beach sand.

Telling time from the beginning.

I swam in the amniotic fluid of life in Bali. Born again opposite of North. Born in the Hindu land of Gods. The night after the zombie death cliffs, I was high on psychedelic mushrooms, beach sunsets, sand graves, grave-ity and starting over.

My life curling and unfurling with the salt and infiniteness in a pool on the beach. The underwater lights changing from red to blue, to green, to yellow, and back to red. Endlessly dancing with color in my watery home. My feet never got tired and my breath never ran out. Tripping, swirling, contained only by the whiteness of the edges.

Whiteness so bright, like the white you see from sudden pain, like a baseball hitting your face when the tears are't there yet.

Whiteness in the night reflecting color. Supernova's in the black. Hadron Colliders and orbits. Black sand on the bottom of the pool swirling with my movements, floating effortless at the top, breathing in the space and stars of the sky with whiteness all around. Diving down below. The emptiness in the center of my chest was filled with color-light and space-water.

The re-knitting of my atoms, the connection of my bones, the fibers of my muscles, all together in one place. It was filled with the infinity of him-dragons and trust, safety and hope, balance and power, truth and lightning.

He held me, I was safe.

We took a breath together.

It was perfect.

ACT IV - Conversations and Cannibalism

**"To walk fully in the light,
one must first be *intimate* with the dark."**

~Peter 'Drago' Tiemann

Judge, Jury and Executioner

Whoever undertakes to set himself up as a judge of Truth and Knowledge is shipwrecked by the laughter of the gods.

~Albert Einstein

Spoiler alert, I live in the end. Sometimes, despite my better judgement. That is, until, I die... which is inevitable. Unless, of course, I am a vampire, in that case I will live forever, but I haven't glittered yet, and I don't burst into flames in the sunshine so, so far so good.

There are a few things in life in which I do really well, one of which is executing a plan. Call it determination, stubbornness, or defiance, perhaps to my own detriment. I executed a death-plan which could only be rivaled by an execution from the Mistress of Death herself. I did die that day on those cliffs. But not in the way I would have imagined.

There are some truths in life and death, the first being, everything about my lies and shame and guilt and expectations died. I finally felt free. Second, when you never plan to come back to the United States, and you do, and you have nothing because everything else in your life has died, nothing is what welcomes you. Nothing. No job, no house, no possessions, no friends, no work, no welcome home party and nothing but your skin and your street-smarts.

It was with this nothingness that for the first time since ... well... since I don't remember when. I felt free. Connected with everything everywhere, and with nothing at the same time. It was not in the religious-fervor or neo-new-age hippy sort of way. But in the peaceful and happy and *I'm okay and actually kind of perfect in all my beautiful imperfections* way.

And depressed.

Grieving the great big hole which was left behind.

Then, to face life with these truths. Plus the truth that, for a very, very long time up until this point, I wasn't a very happy OR NICE person. The first year back was the most difficult, most depressed, and most empty I have ever felt.

So I started writing.

Depression is a lonely, hollow and isolating place. It is grayish black with no color, no edges and no feeling. The black words on white paper gave me some definition. Depression is numbness and everything uninterestingly-ness. It is everything we don't want to address, face and ironically, we don't even know how to respond when someone else is feeling it.

I was a comet lost in space.

In a culture which thrives on conspicuous consumption, I had nothing. Yet, humans have an innate need to search for something with deeper meaning. We dig ourselves little holes just to see what is there. It is a natural process of exploration.

I dated a guy once who was convinced he was going to find buried treasure. He drove all over a mountain top, searched old trails, followed ancient landmarks and dug nearly two dozen six by ten foot holes. He was convinced his gold was just under the next shovel-full of dirt.

Is that what we are doing as Americans? In a society where our culture is assimilation, conforming and consuming. Our culture of impermanence and newness, war and aggression. Of dominance. Are we so starved for something meaningful, real and deep that we will settle for anything? Moving mountains of dirt for just a speck of gold?

I vowed not to collect meaninglessness anymore. But, then... how would I find meaning and joy in starting over in a world full of *stuff*. Starting over with nothing but joy in my heart? Joy which I found 20,000 miles away, but took quite a beating when I stuffed it into my backpack and took it on the journey back to the States. The loss of stuff wasn't the cause of the depression, but perhaps the joy cargo which got beaten in transit was.

Still struggling every day with anxiety and a disfigured version of some demon calling himself Post Traumatic Stress. It is hard to live in a culture which is so aggressive in nature, consuming things, all while fighting anxiety, and emptiness. It was depressingly freeing. You have to remember, I wasn't the girl of the fairytales. I didn't believe in happy endings, I was no fair maiden, and there was no Prince.

Being back in the states and caught between a rock and a hard place. Isn't there a word for that? Oh yes... reality.

The difference was, my life wasn't about escape any more. It wasn't an attempt at emotionally, mentally or spiritually leaving my body for a moment of ecstatic-ness. It was embracing my body. The thing which had betrayed, lied and been used against me. But just because I had good intentions and had this epiphany half-way around the world, didn't magically fix the things that were sharp shards on the insides. It was a struggle.

It still is a struggle. Every single day.

But, the lens I am looking through is different. The lens which once saw darkness and shadows and secrets, now sees hope, even in the darkness.
It sees breath.

It sees all of those things even in moments of impossible, where hopelessness seems imminent. It sees forgiveness of self.

I thought I was broken. I lived a life in which I was cast as a sinner, a black sheep, a shadow, vampire, bitch or mistress. I thought there was something wrong with me. I thought that there had to be something more than just bad luck to have seen the horrors most people who are casting those stones could only imagine.

But, here is the kicker.

The moment of truth.

There is nothing wrong with me. Just like there is nothing wrong with you. You are perfect. Just like me. We are perfect in our imperfections as we float and wade and swim through the waves of life just trying to make some sense of our existence, to find some meaning in our world. Some find it through religion, some through family, some through work and others, like me, find it through our journey into, and out of the darkness. Bad things happen, bad things which change us, hurt us, heal us and make us stronger.
I am strong.

The strongest I have ever been. But it is only through the hottest of fires in the forge does steel gain its strength.

And the truth will set you free....
I will never have children. I can't. My attacker did. He is married now with kids of his own. I know his address and I could have shown up on his doorstep a thousand and one times. I spent hours and days and months envisioning his death. But, it won't happen by my hand. The evil of that day will no longer have a place inside of me to call home. The darkness bred no longer lives in this world, even if he still does.

Here is the hardest truth I can punch with.

I'm sorry.

I am sorry I never said anything so long ago. I'm sorry to those women I found on the streets and offered a job. I'm sorry I hurt you. The stack of cash for you wasn't worth it.

I know.

I am sorry to the men I prodded to hurt me. I wanted everything to be your fault. I hated you before you met me because I hated me. It was the only defense mechanism I had. It was the only thing I knew. It was my fucked up normal.

I'm sorry to me. I will never treat myself that way again.

That girl died on the cliffs.

I have decided I won't get married again. For a variety of complex and personal reasons I am not yet ready to share. But, that doesn't mean I won't love to the deepest part of my soul. Because, right now, I am in the middle of finding that love at the bottom, in the middle, in the wet and amongst the stars. A cosmic love with an orbit.

I don't believe in one singular Almighty. But that doesn't mean I'm not a good person who does good things.

It is through these deepest have-not's in which we find what we do truly have.

I struggled with even the idea to write this. But, until I set my experiences down on paper, until I spent the time to ponder the perfect words to describe it, I couldn't fully appreciate or understand it. Threading related experiences together, I started to see a pattern in the quilt of my own existence. A quilt to keep me warm on rainy days. And... it has rained a lot. So my quilt grew, and gained more threads of color and texture. It holds hearts and lies and dreams and secrets and truth. It is welcoming and open and big enough for everyone who wants to snuggle and watch the lightning storms and rains from a safe place. This quilt will never judge you for what you have done, what you have gone through or how you have dealt with it.

My point is, you are never alone in your struggles. I struggled silently, alone in the dark, underwater and afraid. Most drownings happen that way. Silently. Most drownings do not have the violent splashing or screams for help. Drowning is usually a deceptively quiet event. I've known that since I worked as a Lifeguard so many summers ago. The respiratory system is designed for breathing, speech is secondary.

Breathing MUST be fulfilled before speech can occur.

And yet.... I still didn't recognize it when it was happening to me.

Sometimes bad things happen to good people. Sometimes, those bad things change those people, and sometimes, the strength which is shown from those changes isn't apparent until they are finished creating their own quilt.

On my travels I was gifted a piece of gold. A small pressed piece of gold with an inlay of Quan Yin riding a Dragon. This little memento is significant. Quan Yin is the East Asian Buddhist Goddess of Compassion/Mercy. A Bodhisattva, Enlightened Being or Immortal in Chinese Taoist beliefs. She is riding my Malifecent. My dragon. She has not only raised and commanded all the powers of dark and light and everything in between, but she does so gracefully on the back of a dragon. She is serene while she guides the ferocity of this dragon through the deep tumultuous waves. I see this now as a metaphor for my journey over the years. To attain the stance of mastery over turbulent happenings. To tame my own inner dragons when they surface amidst the upheavals in life. Riding the rolling waves gracefully, with serenity in the face of chaotic circumstances.

Choices are determined by attitude, not by the events themselves, and our outer posture is decided by the inner stance of our attitude and determination. Strength, balance, self-mastery—all these qualities are depicted in Quan Yin's graceful bearing atop the dragon. She is unmoved by the fierceness of the creature or the swirling of the waves. She is in command of herself, peaceful in her stance and competent in her mode of travel and the forces of nature around her. Quan Yin and her dragon ended up as the symbol of the transformational process which inevitably happened by this journey. The dragon itself represents primal forces which were tamed, and when they are tamed, they bring good fortune.

The kind woman who gave this piece of gold to me, did so by just laying it in front of the door of my room while I was sleeping. In the silence of night, shrouded by darkness, surrounded by the nightmare and bloodlust of Cambodia, the Goddess of Compassion and Mercy lay at my threshold and good fortune has been by my side ever since.

This small piece of gold, this dragon travels with me. It will be with me long after I die and my flesh turns to dust. My reminder that the human will is strong. It is defiant. It has the power to laugh in the face of danger, defy the odds and drink in all of life's pleasures without the gluttonous-overload that make a stomach suffer and sour. It desires to explore with great curiosity, to innovate and create. It has the power to change the world. Gracefully. Peacefully. Beautifully.

You know that feeling when you walk into a room and it seems as though everyone is holding their breath? Well, Earth walked into a Universe like that, a Universe just waiting to exhale. Waiting to exhale and celebrate your accomplishments, despite all the cards which were stacked against you.

Take a breath, because your Universe just exhaled...

...And all the stars are sparkling.

Gods and Sharks

"Live a good life.
If there are Gods and they are just,
then they will not care how devout you have been,
but will welcome you
based on the virtues you have lived by.
If there are Gods, but unjust,
then you should not want to worship them.
If there are no Gods, then you will be gone, but will
have lived a noble life that will live on in the memories
of your loved ones."

~Marcus Aurelius

Somewhere along the line I started telling stories, and
people would laugh, raise their eyebrows and tell me to
write a book all in the same breath. So I did. I started to
write something that resembles a book. The writing forced
an incredible amount of introspection on an already very
introspective being.

Lost into a sea, swimming with my memories, emotions and self-made sharks. I had to get really honest with myself about everything. Being brutally honest with myself about choices and failures was not that easy, nor was revisiting my feelings to experience them again and again until I was no longer a prisoner of war. I was still drowning, swimming with the sharks that would nip at my heals, and all the years I spent training in a pool did not prepare me for this. Although, in all the years I spent anchoring the relay, I knew I would have to dive into the shallow end, the end which had big red signs that said **No Diving**.

So, I dove. Headfirst. I wrote, re-lived and held my breath, one last time.

It's one thing to write it in the privacy of my own home, my own room... to write with no intention of ever letting anyone else read it. To write about everything, to put it on paper and see it in front of me. Then to realize that eventually there would be other people to see it, read it and at some level I had to deal with their disappointments, judgements and shame cast in my direction almost deterred me from writing anything.

But, protecting other people is where all the trouble started. The arrogance of performing and deciding what another person needs or wants to hear.

It didn't stop the fear, and in fact was downright terrifying. It was by far the hardest thing I have ever done in my life. The process was marred with sleepless nights and anxiety fueled days. Pulling out each little tarnished broken and wounded piece of my soul to inspect, analyze, hold, comfort and repair. To cry and scream and laugh and share. The process was bittersweet, healing and completely took over my life. I was, at times, more difficult to live with than an uncaged, hungry and very rabid tiger.

In the shallow end of the pool.

When our mind remembers, our soul, emotions and sub-conscious re-live those memories. Our bodies respond to the electrical impulses and stress happens. Stress based upon memories, emotions, fears and lies. They are all subconscious triggers which are not happening in physicality exactly at that moment, but are felt in the body none-the-less.

In this journey, I found there were specific types of people which naturally gravitated closer during my journey. It was those people who never judged, those who opened their arms for hugs when I needed, food when I was hungry and words of encouragement when I was blue. These were the people who never would look at me like some pitied victim, but instead, the people who would just look at me and say,

"Good job."

Help me dust the dirt from my knees.

Help me put my shoes back on, and help me take the first step again.

Those steps with my fresh, new, little land feet.

Those are the people to surround yourself with. Those who are not just human, not just mere mortals. In my world, God doesn't live out there or in heaven. It is not some far-off deity. But walks the earth. A God held in the soul of every single person. A goodness that lives deep inside each of us. The goodness of mere mortal Gods which spit on the Mistress of Death willfully and defy the very odds and negativity in which this culture programs us to believe.

Gods which live and laugh and love...

... and breathe underwater.

Gods which leave notes behind for us to find when we feel as though we have nothing left to hold on to. Gods in the shape of beloved Grandmothers.

October 31, 1994

What a great opportunity you have to be associated with such a fine group and to experience all the fellowship it offers. Hopefully, the friends you make now will remain with you for a long, long time; therefore it is so important to choose wisely.

You have been blessed with both beauty and brains – that gives you a unique advantage. Quite a few people would like to set higher goals, but do not have the capacity to do so. In your case you are not restricted – you have the ability to accomplish whatever goal you choose.

Many years ago, when I was younger than you are now, we had autograph books in which friends and relatives wrote little sayings. My grandmother Waterman wrote the following in my book and I will pass it along to you.

"Lost: Somewhere between sunrise and sunset sixty golden minutes each set with sixty diamond seconds. No reward is offered for they are gone forever."

Just remember that I love you and want the best for you in whatever you choose and will always be there to help you in that choice.

Lots of Love,
Grandma Phyllis

A year after she penned this letter, I was raped. Five years after that, she died. Ten years after that, the Dragon-man said yes. It all happened in the same month of orbit.

October.

Seems like it happens all at the same time, rather than separated by a span of 15 years. I guess space and time are funny that way. Spinning and orbiting, darting in and out and playing like evil little time-trick toddlers on the playground inside our mind. The stars aligning in some Universal orbit to collide at particular repetitive moments, leading us to our climactic points.

October is my climactic point. A month of death and performances, thunderstorms and perfect Indian summers. A month of ghouls, crispy pies and see-through leaves.

The climactic points which test our strength, test our resolve, and test our belief.

If you believe in God, then you have to believe in me.

Crossed Legs and Coffee

*"When you are truly honest and revealing about
yourself, it creates a sigh in other people.
They realize they are not alone, they are not a freak:
Someone else has felt the exact same way or lived their
dream If you are going to skimp on the truth, then you
are doing a disservice.
Honesty is not only a gift to other people -
it is a gift to yourself."*

~Lorna Kelly

Let's sit down together and have one final cup of coffee.
Cross our legs under the table and reflect on what we
have lived through together. Swirls of milk and coffee
look very similar no matter how old you are, where in the
world you are or what time of day it is. The dark and
light dancing in the creamy wet. The dance of silence and
good conversation.

You have read this book and seen me at my most naked.
Seen me drowning at the bottom of the pool. You have
watched me flail in the deep bluest of blacks, thrash and

gasp for breath in the waves, and been there as I somehow figure my way back to the surface, walking from the ocean like a Siren, pearls in hand.

For Halloween one year I went as a *little white lie* and I dressed all in black. The fun part of the night, and the brilliance of the costume was, every person I saw I asked them to tell me their little secrets, their little white lies. I collected many many secrets that night dressed as *Post Secret* in the flesh. But the depth and intelligence of the costume wasn't the secrets, the whiteness or the dressing in all black. It was knowing that whatever secrets I encountered on this night of ghouls and goblins, those secrets could never be as bad as the ones I already kept.

There is healing in expunging the secrets of your soul. In shedding the weight of self-imposed shame. And, finishing this memoir is, in effect, handing my life over to you. Handing my life over to the world. Saying,

"This is what I went through, this is who I am and maybe you can learn something from it."

Hoping that perhaps you can receive some glimpse of wisdom and benefit from my experience without having to actually live through the horrors. I found tremendous healing in this experience. Not in the *time heals all wounds* sort of bull-shit, but the healing that comes with being able to trace the footsteps and know that I never have to re-live any of it again. Healing that happens when you realize the strength which you never believed in before is now sitting in front of you in black and white.

And honestly... I don't give a shit if these words sell. I don't care about book success or publishing deals or book tours. What I care about is that these words are written. That these words are spoken. That the truth is set free. I care that the performance is over, and the lights are turned up.

Until I found this truth, I never found the connection I so desperately craved. Living in such a hurried world that to stop and pay attention, the opening of the soul and caring must happen. The deeper the care, the longer the attention in our short little lives. The longer the attention, the deeper the impact in our souls.

The story just isn't about me, but about every single person who feels as though they don't have a voice. A lot of people struggle in silence about something. Not wanting to bother anyone, not wanting to make a big deal, too afraid to be seen as weak or whiney. Whatever the reason is, it silences us. Silences us because we are so completely focused on gasping for air. We are drowning and can't call out. Those who are screaming, are doing it underwater and no one can hear them. For the few of us who breathe, there are a thousand others that drown.

You have seen me running and swimming because it was so much easier that facing the monsters. Giving up everything, no less than my life in totality, was easier than facing the demons. But, to stick with the honesty, I was first and perhaps always will be, a lifeguard, even in the midst of my drowning.

I have lived much of my life submerged. Coated in wet and blood and shame. The dark is intimate and the shadows are much less scary when you know who is casting them.

Sometimes people hold their breath for so long, you think they can breathe underwater.

In this small little diatribe I have affectionately named a memoir, I have left many, many stories out. Many secrets have still yet gone unshared, many conversations have yet to be had, it is just words written on a puddle at this point. I am okay with that. Because when our words fail us, because sometimes they do, we will always have the water.

The clear blue.

The water is our home. It holds us, changes us and heals us. It is our truest form and our perfect reflection. It is where it all began, and where it will all end. All we have to do is take a breath at some point in the middle.

I believe in that more than anything.

About the Author

Rae Jones once sprung from the wild deserts of Eastern Oregon, was raised on a liquid diet of business savvy, money management and stress in Portland, Oregon.

She has been spotted in exotic locations like Indonesia, Mexico, Japan, Canada and the always mysterious United States of America.

A self-proclaimed coffee aficionado and champagne sipper, this author and adventure provocateur has a PhD in learning life lessons the hard way.

In her spare time she channels all of her excess jittery energy and butterfly-length attention span into ideas of how to leave footprints on all the sandy beaches of the world.